How to Use a Computer
to Improve Your Business

Other Titles in the Better Business Series

How to Start and Run Your Own Business, 7th edition, 1989,
M. Mogano

How to Start and Run Your Own Shop, 2nd edition, 1988, P. Levene

How to Give a Successful Presentation, 1988, I. Richards

The Shopkeeper's Handbook, 1989, P. Levene

How to Get a Better Job, 1989, M. Mogano

The Husband and Wife Business Partnership: What the Law Says, 1989,
D. and M. Owles

Front cover design by, Jill Turner, Amstrad plc.

Better Business Series

How to Use a Computer to Improve Your Business

Ian Richards

Graham & Trotman

A member of the Kluwer Academic Publishers Group
LONDON/DORDRECHT/BOSTON

First published in 1989 by

Graham & Trotman Limited
Sterling House
66 Wilton Road
London SW1V 1DE
UK

Graham & Trotman Inc
Kluwer Academic Publishers Group
101 Philip Drive
Assinippi Park
Norwell, MA 02061
USA

ISBN 1 85333 323 9 (Paperback)
ISBN 1 85333 324 7 (Hardback)
1 85333 088 4 (Series)
© I. Richards, 1989

British Library Cataloguing in Publication Data

Richards, Ian
   How to use a computer to improve your business.
   1. Business firms. Applications of computer systems
   I. Title   II. Series
   658'.05

   ISBN 1 85333 324 7
   ISBN 1 85333 323 9 pbk

Library of Congress Cataloging in Publication Data

Richards, Ian
   How to use a computer to improve your business / I. Richards
      p.   cm. —— (Better business series)
   ISBN 1-85333-324-7. —— ISBN 1-85333-323-9 (pbk.)
   1. Business — Data processing.   2. Microcomputers.   3. Small
business — Data processing.   I. Title.   II. Series.
HF5548.2.R486   1989
650'.028'5416 — dc20   89–25998
                                                CIP

Computer typeset by author
Printed and bound in Great Britain by
Billing & Sons Ltd, Worcester

Contents

Preface

Is technology leaving you behind?

You may think that a computer is an extravagance you can do without. What's the point of spending money on a machine that you don't understand if you are doing quite nicely without one?

But what would you think if a shopkeeper in your street used a bucket instead of a till? What a fool! How could he be sure that his takings were right? No proper records - he'd be asking for trouble.

Or if a friend of yours went into business, how would you advise him to record his takings and expenses? In a cash book split up into columns? Why? Because it makes life easier at the end of the day.

And if the shopkeeper down the road ignored your advice to use a till, because it was too expensive; or if your friend going into business said he wouldn't use a proper cashbook because he "Didn't understand accounts", you'd think, rightly, that both were being pig-headed to their own disadvantage.

When it comes to computers, it's easy to fall into the same trap yourself.

There is nothing special or mysterious about computers. They are tools which help make life easier. Just as a till helps you control your takings, or a proper cash book helps you keep your accounts straight, a computer can help you in any number of other ways.

However, to be fair, there are problems with computers that don't apply to things like tills and cash books.

Firstly, they are complex machines. Whereas you can see and understand what a cash book or a till does, it's not so clear with a computer. Part of this problem arises because computers are so immensely flexible that they can be used for all sorts of things.

Secondly, there is so much jargon floating about with computers that the average man in the street can be blinded by science before the salesman has got half way through the first sentence, "You see sir, the real advantage of this machine lies in its 32 bit processor operating at a speed of 20MHz, an obvious improvement on its main competitor". Really? But how does that help you sell shoes? Repair cars? Or go about whatever business you happen to be in? Not so obvious.

Hundreds, perhaps thousands of businesses have been sold computers by slick salesmen, only to find them gathering dust, because they don't know how to use them. Worse, some businesses have invested large amounts of time and money in buying machinery, developing systems, training staff, to find out months later that the computer is unusable, because it fails to meet a basic requirement of the business.

The pitfalls are there - as countless numbers of bitter businessmen will testify.

This book has been written to help you. It will explain simply and clearly what a computer is and how it can be used. It provides a safe guide through the jungle of over-eager jargon-oozing salesmen. It will take you step by step through the stages of assessing your needs, choosing a computer, setting up your systems and keeping things running smoothly. And if you follow the methods explained in this book you will avoid the traps that can put your business at risk.

Thousands of businesses have been improved beyond recognition by introducing computers. In some cases ailing companies have been turned into highly successful concerns.

Don't stagnate. Keep your eye where the action is. And make your business a winner!

Ian Richards,

Goshawk Ltd.,
96, Goshawk Gardens,
Hayes,
Middlesex UB4 8LD.

(01) 845 0145

1st, September 1989.

Introduction

The approach taken in this book is to guide you through the stages of buying a computer and improving your systems in the same order that you will carry them out.

First, we will look at how a computer can be used. We will consider the kind of things that you need to do to run your business and consider whether a computer could be used to make life easier. This will give us some idea of what we are working towards.

Once we have looked at the possible uses of computers, we will look at the nature of the beast itself. It is perhaps not strictly necessary to know anything about computers and still be able to run a computer application successfully year in - year out. But the more you know the better placed you are to make decisions; and the less likely you are to be taken in by the jargon-oozing salesmen.

So we will go through the basics of what a computer is. You won't learn enough to sit a degree in computer science - but you will be able to speak intelligently about computers to your fellow businessmen and be able to make informed decisions about your own business.

Once we have covered the technical aspect, we will turn our attention to your business. How do you go about deciding whether an application is suitable for computerization? How can you be sure what the real needs of the business are?

We will look at the various methods of analysing your needs and get a clear idea of how your business can be helped. After all, we are not computerizing for the sake of it - in the long term it has to make the business more profitable.

When you have identified your needs, decision time approaches. Which machine to pick? What is the relevance of software and hardware? All will be explained!

We will find out how to introduce a new system at minimum risk to the continuing trade of the business.

When the system is installed, how do you make sure it stays running smoothly? We will examine the techniques.

Finally, we will look into the future. How will you know when the present system has outlived its usefulness? How do you set about upgrading? And, to conclude, what are the most important lessons we have covered in this book?

So there, your course is mapped out. Have a pleasant journey!

CHAPTER 1

How Can a Computer Help?

Quite clearly, there are limits to what a computer will do. If you are a market trader, the computer won't stand on an apple box for you and enthral the masses with a quick, witty sales patter. But the day will come...

So, the area we are looking at is the businessman's favourite moan, the 'paperwork'. There are two ways in which the computer could help:

1. By making existing jobs easier.
2. By enabling you to introduce new procedures which can improve the general efficiency of the business.

Let's look at an example of each.

What sort of job could a computer make easier? An obvious example that springs to mind is the preparation of wage dockets. The manual procedure might be to take the employees' hours at standard time and multiply by the rate. Then take the hours worked at overtime rate and multiply by the overtime rate. Then add the figures together to get Gross pay and work out all the deductions for income tax, national insurance, pension, etc. And finally, prepare a wage docket showing all the relevant figures.

A computer system could be introduced so that all you have to do is enter the hours worked for each employee, and the computer will then automatically calculate all the figures and print off the wage dockets. A major improvement if wages happen to be one of your favourite bugbears.

That's an example of how to make a job easier, but how can a computer improve efficiency? How could the introduction of new procedures be a help? Surely the idea is to cut down on the paperwork, not create more of it?

Yes, but...

Some procedures can bring great benefits at the expense of very little time. Say, for example, that you presently keep your records of suppliers and customers on card index files. You can check on the position for an individual supplier or customer quite quickly, but it's not so easy to know what your overall position is at any one time. And how about payments? Are you sure that all of your customers are not extending their credit? Do you use credit given to you to the full?

If you kept your supplier and customer records on computer you could introduce a few simple procedures to help improve your cash flow. For instance, payments to suppliers could be done on the basis of a weekly list produced by the computer. The list would show only those invoices for which the credit period is about to expire, so that no payments are made until necessary.

On the customer side, a list could be produced monthly showing the outstanding balance for all customers. The balance would be split into columns showing how much of the total was two months old, three months old, etc. In this way you can chase up all your outstanding debts much more often. And you will be able to see at a glance which customers are taking liberties and concentrate your fire on those. Reports such as this often give an early indication of firms in financial trouble, and quick action on your part can considerably reduce your bad debt costs.

Once a system is installed, procedures such as these can be carried out at the touch of a button. Not a significant additional burden for the benefits it produces.

And it doesn't stop there. We have just plucked examples out of the air. For your business, the requirements might be different. But the possibilities are waiting to be explored.

Of course, this book cannot tell you what the best approach for your business is. We will look at the general requirements of most businesses, and from this you will recognize the features that are particularly relevant to you. You may think that you have a business which is too individual to be catered for by this approach. But read on, you will be surprised at how similar the needs of a variety of businesses are.

It may be that the special requirements of your business suggest that a specialist package would be suitable, or you may even need something produced specifically for your business. We will consider these instances in Chapter 6 when we discuss the whole subject of choosing a system in much greater depth. Suffice it to say that for smaller businesses the trend is to rely on the wide range of general purpose packages which are already on the market. In general, the paperwork requirements of a business revolve around three major activities:

1. Producing documents such as letters, invoices, advice notes, contracts, etc.
2. Storing information - almost everything has to be filed, and it must be done in such a way that it can be retrieved easily. Customer and supplier names and addresses, details of individual invoices, descriptions of the products you sell, information on stock levels; these are all possible examples.
3. Accounting. Nearly all the activities of the business require some kind of figure work: working out margins, prices, profits, etc.

Because these needs are so widespread, general purpose packages have been developed to assist each function. These are:

For document production:	The Word Processor.
For filing:	The Database.
For accounting:	The Spreadsheet and General Accounts packages.

In this chapter we will look briefly at what these packages can do. In Chapter 4 we will study them in depth.

The Word Processor

A word processor could be described as the ultimate refinement of the electronic typewriter. Its main purpose is to produce printed output on a sheet of paper. But the flexibility it lends to accomplishing this task is immense.

Originally word processors were sold separately from computers, as all-inclusive units, but this is rare today, the preference being to buy a word processing package which can be run on a general purpose computer.

So: How is a word processor used? What can it do?

The main difference between a typewriter and a word processor is that instead of typing directly onto a sheet of paper, the text is typed on the computer keyboard and, as it is typed, displayed on the computer screen. The text of the document is stored by the computer, and you can call it up on screen at any time. When the document is finished, it can be printed off on a printer attached to the computer.

Your first reaction to this might be that it is a step backwards. With a typewriter the document is ready immediately, but with a computer you have to wait for it to be printed.

It has to be admitted that a typewriter can be quicker than a word processor. But, this is only true if:

1. You never make a typing mistake.
2. You never require more than one good copy of a document.

The beauty of a word processor is that, because you can see the document on the screen, you can proof read it, edit it, change your mind about what you want to say, and then, only when you are satisfied, print off the document. With a typewriter, to correct a mistake you have to re-type the whole document; with a word processor you only have to change the part that you got wrong. You can add words, delete words, correct spelling mistakes, move paragraphs around, do virtually anything you like. And the 'final draft' is the only one that need be printed. And if you do need more than one copy, you can print as many additional copies as you want, whenever you like.

In circumstances where a document has to be agreed by a third party, you can produce the first draft, send it off for review, and then just make the requisite changes before printing off the final copy. For a hefty document this can save hours of re-typing, draft after draft.

Most word processors offer a host of other facilities. For instance, say that you were looking through a particularly long document for the words 'Super-dynamo bung plug' the word processor can be instructed to search for the phrase and take you to that part of the document immediately. And then if you needed to change 'Super-dynamo bung plug' to 'Superfill bung-plugger' the word processor can be instructed to search through the entire document and exchange every occurrence.

Word processors are very good for producing 'standard' documents, like contracts. All the standard clauses can be pre-prepared on a 'template' document, so that a contract can be produced quickly by copying the template, filling in the appropriate details, and printing it.

Another, less obvious, advantage is that it will probably lure you into picking up some typing skills. Most businessmen, who wouldn't dream of sitting behind a typewriter, show much more interest in a computer. And if you are using the computer for other things why not prepare documents as well? Word processing is not like typing. You can write a sentence, read it, go back over it, make changes, read it again... It becomes a much more interactive process. And because you can see what you have just written, it can help clarify what you think as you write. You may be sceptical about the prospect of doing your own typing, but it can produce considerable savings in the long run, and... just wait until you get your new toy!

The Database

What a horrible word! If ever a term was invented to put ordinary people off computers 'database' must surely be it.

You may hear many complicated explanations of what a database is. Jargon words abound, 'relational', 'hierarchical', 'multi-dimensional', '4th generation language'.

What a load of codswallop!

A database is nothing more than the computer equivalent of a filing cabinet. A very useful type of filing cabinet, but that is all.

So what advantages does a computer-type filing cabinet have over the ordinary kind? (There must be some, or we wouldn't be talking about it.)

The big difference is this: with an ordinary filing cabinet, information can only be referenced in one way. For instance, records of supplier details might be held in a card index in alphabetical order. If you needed to know all the suppliers that lived in Slough, or all the suppliers which sold tobacco, you wouldn't be able to find out unless you went through all the records in the card index, listing them out by hand.

With a database system, you don't have that problem. It's as if you had a card index file referenced in alphabetical order, that at the same time was also referenced in order of location, and was also referenced in order of product type. In fact, you can access the information in any order you like. With a card index this would be physically impossible. You can only put one set of cards in one order. But with information stored by the computer, those sort of restrictions don't apply.

You can ask for information according to almost any criteria. For example, show me all the customers that live in Basingstoke with outstanding balances over £2,000. Or, show me all the information on file for the supplier whose name is F.M. Bloggs. Or, show me all the details for wholesalers supplying foodstuffs and clothing. And because the information is held in the computer, it can be used to print off reports. If your usual practice is to prepare a list of debtors each month, with a database system you could just as quickly run off two lists, one in order of supplier, and one in order of amount, highlighting your major debtors.

The ways in which you can use a database system are almost endless. Suppose, for instance, you are a newsagent. You have just started stocking a new magazine offering investment advice. You wish to promote an introductory offer, but you have only a limited number of leaflets. How do you decide which houses to send the literature to? With a database system it would be easy to request a list of customers ordering the quality papers, say, the *Times, Guardian* and *Telegraph.* The database system will also be able to print off address labels. If you have a word processing system, you can link to the database system and automatically produce a series of letters, individually addressed to each prospective customer. 'Dear Mr. Smith' sounds much better than 'Dear Sir or Madam'. And remember, you type the letter once only, the computer automatically produces the rest from the information provided by the database system.

Now you may not be a newsagent promoting a new magazine, but can you think of a similar application for your business where a database system would be useful?

The Spreadsheet

A spreadsheet is a sort of advanced calculator. It can be used whenever calculations are performed using a pre-set format. Perhaps the best way to explain is to use a few examples.

```
                          INVOICE

   From:

   Hi-technic bargains
   Cheaptelly Way,
   Snowscreen City.

    Date:              Ref:

   Qty.    Item                        Unit price      Total
                                                         £
           26" Supercon TV             125.00
           20" Medcon TV                95.00
           14" Minicon Colour TV        65.00
           Mugsbuyit HK Video          199.00

           Subtotal:

           VAT:

           Amount due:                              £_____
```

Figure 1.1

Consider the pro-forma invoice in Figure 1.1. To use the invoice in practice, you first need to fill in the quantity for each product ordered, then multiply by the unit price to get the total for each product, then add up to get the overall subtotal, then work out the VAT amount, and finally, add the VAT amount to the subtotal to get the amount due.

If you used a spreadsheet system, none of the calculations would be necessary. You would simply fill in the quantity for each product ordered. The computer would work out all the figures and print off the invoice.

Another example of the use of a spreadsheet, is the Cash flow calculation. Consider the following example:

	JAN	FEB	MAR	APR	MAY	JUN
IN HAND	600	****	****	***	****	****
Sales	3200	2000	2600	3100	2900	1900
Other	300	300	300	300	300	300
INCOME	****	****	****	****	****	****
Wages	800	800	800	950	950	950
Rent	900	900	900	900	1000	1000
Purchases	2000		2900		700	
EXPENSES	****	****	****	****	****	****
GAIN/LOSS	****	****	****	****	****	****
IN HAND	****	****	****	****	****	****

The cash flow pro-forma is used to calculate what the likely level of future cash balances is going to be. The figures put in are estimates of future income and expenses. The spaces marked by asterisks represent totals which can be worked out from the other figures.

In practice, if you prepared a cash flow statement such as this, it wouldn't take long to work out the total figures. But then: What if wages went up by more than you thought? or: What if sales were lower than expected?

To find out you would need to prepare a whole new sheet from scratch. But if you used a spreadsheet things would be different. On a spreadsheet, the computer works out all the totals. So if you decide to change, say, the wages figure, all the totals figures on the spreadsheet will change immediately to show the new figures. You can make as many changes as you like, asking 'What if?', and the computer will show you, immediately, the effect on your cash balance.

Of course, invoices and cash flow statements are not the only use of spreadsheets. They can be used for month end accounts, tax calculations, working out discounts; in fact any job where you need to calculate something following a pre-set format.

Using the Products Available

The systems we have looked at in this chapter can best be described as utilities. They do not enable you to run a fully integrated, computerized system, but they provide the facilities needed to take care of the most commonly occurring office needs. Most businesses could buy one of these packages tomorrow, and start to derive some benefit from using it within a few months.

But that is not the way forward. If you really want to get the most out of computers, a considered approach is far more sensible. For example, you may be tempted to rush out and buy a spreadsheet, only to discover later that you would be much better off with a general accounts package.

A general accounts package is a product which will handle all your bookkeeping functions for you. Most commercial packages come in separate modules i.e., Bought ledger, Sales ledger, Payroll, Cashbook, Nominal ledger, Stock.

The good packages are 'integrated', so that, for example, if you run your bought ledger processing, it will then automatically update the nominal ledger figures. These modular packages can be useful as they allow you to start by using just one of the modules and then build up gradually to a full system.

General packages of this sort are not confined only to accounting systems. There may be something available that caters for the specific needs of your type of business.

Your eventual business solution may consist of using a general package together with some utility programs all integrated smoothly with your manual procedures. Then your business will be able to shed some of its fat and gain a significant benefit from technology.

But this happy state of affairs is not reached by accident. Throughout the rest of this book we will give you the knowledge to get there by design. We start this process in the next chapter by covering some technical groundwork, asking the question: What is a computer?

Summary of Chapter 1 - How Can a Computer Help?

In this chapter we have looked at the general needs of a business in terms of clerical functions. These are:

1. Producing documents.
2. Filing.
3. Accounting.

We have seen how each of these functions can be assisted by the use of:

1. Word Processors.
2. Database systems.
3. Spreadsheets and Accounting Packages.

CHAPTER 2

What is a Computer?

In this chapter we will look closely at what a computer is. We will start off with a very general, high-level look. Then we will go on to make a detailed examination of the machine and how it works. We will look at the workings of a computer in far greater detail than you would ever need to know when using one in practice. But the aim of this chapter is to give you a good understanding of how computers work. You will then be better equipped to make decisions. Many businessmen think they know something about computers, but in many cases, what they know amounts to little more than a collection of half-baked analogies. And in some cases that can be more of a hindrance than a help. A little knowledge is a dangerous thing.

Some of the material in this chapter may strike you as being excessively technical. But this impression is more likely to be caused by unfamiliarity with the subject matter, than any inherent conceptual difficulty with the material. As you gain familiarity with the jargon, so the concepts will fall into place. It is worth making the effort to do this, because you will never again feel lost when you are surrounded by technology, or confronted by a crass salesman who tries to blind you with science.

Let's start then by answering the question: What is a computer? According to the Shorter Oxford English Dictionary:

> **Computer**. A calculating-machine; esp. an automatic electronic device for performing mathematical or other operations; frequently with defining word prefixed, as, analogue, digital, electronic computer. Hence *Computerize*, to prepare for operation by, or to operate by means of, a computer.

Not a narrow definition, it encompasses an abacus, a schoolboy's calculator, a digital watch, a till, hand held machines used by journalists and salesmen to record information as they travel, desktop machines used by small businesses, machines the size of a chest freezer linked to several users simultaneously, huge machines connected to terminals all over the world accessed by several thousand people at once, the batteries of machines used by NASA to calculate how a man could reach the moon, and the super fast machines used to interpret huge volumes of climatic data and predict the weather. All of these can be described, legitimately, as computers.

But we will concentrate our attention on the sort of machine that is suitable for a small business; the sort of machine that is likely to useful to you. These machines are called **Personal Computers** (PCs) or **Micro-computers**. (Larger machines called **Mini-computers** and **Mainframes** are used by big companies. The biggest of these can cost many millions of pounds.)

Let's start by looking at the main components of a Personal Computer.

The Personal Computer

A typical Personal Computer (PC) is illustrated in Figure 2.1. There are three main parts:

1. A System Unit (a box, containing the bulk of the electronics).
2. A Monitor (similar to a TV screen).
3. A Keyboard (similar to a typewriter keyboard, with some extra keys).

The monitor and keyboard are both connected by leads to the System Unit. Power leads from both the monitor and the System Unit lead to a normal wall plug socket.

A computer is a general purpose machine that can carry out any number of tasks. How does the computer know what you want to use it for? You must load the appropriate set of instructions into the computer. These sets of instructions are in a special form, which the machine can understand. A set of instructions is called a Program. Computers cannot read instructions from a sheet of paper. Computer instructions are kept on Disks.

Disks come in two types:

1. Floppy disks.
2. Hard disks.

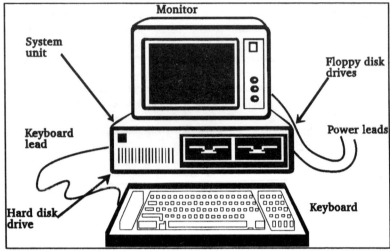

Figure 2.1

A floppy disk (see Figure 2.2) is a thin, circular piece of flexible plastic material held in a square case. The surface of the disk is covered in a magnetic material, similar to that covering a normal cassette tape. The floppy disk is inserted into a slot called a Disk Drive. There is a hole in the square casing so that the 'heads' on the computer's disk drive can access the magnetic surface of the floppy disk. On the more modern types of disk, there is a spring-loaded protective covering around the hole in the disk casing, so that the delicate magnetic material is exposed only when the disk is inserted into the drive. The computer can read information from the disk, or write information onto the disk in the same way that sound can be played from, or recorded onto, a cassette.

The material stored on a floppy disk is organized into Files. Some files may contain programs (sets of instructions for the computer to run), other files may contain data (for example, a list of names and addresses for all your suppliers).

A hard disk functions in much the same way as a floppy disk, the differences being:

1. Instead of being inserted into a disk drive when required, a hard disk is permanently connected to the computer (often contained within the System unit).
2. Hard disks have a much greater capacity than floppy disks.

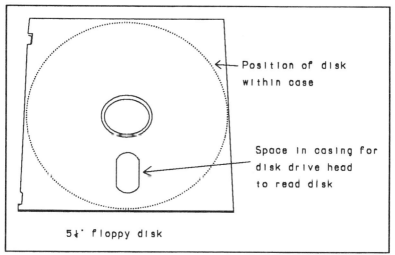

Figure 2.2

When using a PC, the normal mode of operation is as follows. A floppy disk containing the required program is inserted into the disk drive. The user types the name of the required program on the keyboard (this is echoed on the monitor screen). The computer loads the program from the disk. Subsequent actions depend on the nature of the program. Sometimes menus will be shown on the screen and the user will respond, selecting options by typing in letters at the keyboard. Programs for more advanced users may require the user to type in requests in a special type of 'language'. In most cases, as the program runs interaction will take place between the user and the machine, with the relevant information being displayed on the monitor. This element of interactivity is perhaps one of the most useful features of computers; you type in a query, and the computer responds with an answer. There is no time-consuming searching of files to get what you need. And if your query involves a calculation, more time is saved. Even the most basic computers can perform calculations at speeds that seem staggering to the inexperienced user.

This describes how a computer is used. But how does it work? To get a more complete picture, it is perhaps best to start at the lowest level and work up. What goes on in that mysterious box full of electronics? Before we tackle that, let's prepare ourselves with a little background knowledge.

Analogue and Digital systems

In the definition of a computer at the beginning of this chapter, you may have noticed the words analogue and digital. These terms were common in the early days of computers, but now nearly all modern electronic devices are digital, and so the distinction has become redundant. But understanding the concept of a digital process, is central to understanding how a computer works. So we will begin this section by looking at the difference between an analogue and a digital machine.

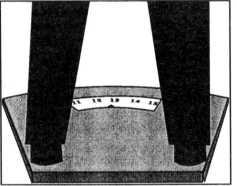

Figure 2.3

An analogue machine works on a *proportional* basis. The result of an analogue operation will depend on the way in which some factor varies in relation to another factor. Digital machines work on a discrete basis. The result of an operation will depend on whether something is there, or is not there. This distinction is more clearly illustrated by example.

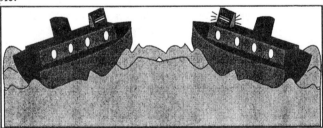

Figure 2.4

Consider for a moment the bathroom scales shown in Figure 2.3. When somebody stands on the scales, a spring is compressed, and the gauge turns to register the weight. Because the amount of turn is always the same for a given weight (within a certain amount of tolerance), the scales can be calibrated, and thereafter relied upon to give reasonably consistent results. The amount of compression, and the angle of turn are *proportional* to the weight on the scale and therefore the scales can be thought of as an *analogue* device.

In the early days of communication, voice transmission was not always reliable, or secure. Telegraph messages were sent using morse code (a regular pattern of long and short buzzes), and ships at sea, with no other means of communicating (or wishing to maintain radio silence) used flashing beacons to communicate (Figure 2.4). Messages sent like this do not depend on the intensity of the signal (the loudness of the sound, or the brightness of the light). It is the pattern that conveys the message. These systems are much less likely to suffer from errors in transmission. It is difficult to make sense out of a muffled voice on a bad line, but detecting the presence or absence of a buzz, or flashing light, is a lot easier. Because the buzzer, or light, can have only two states ('on' or 'off'), these means of communication could be thought of as *digital* devices.

Perhaps the simplest example of a digital device would be an ordinary domestic light - it can only have two states, on or off. But a light with a dimmer switch would be an analogue device - the strength of the light is proportional to the amount turned by the switch.

What is the main advantage of a digital device? There is less likelihood of error. The accuracy of bathroom scales varies with height above sea level. And as time passes and the spring deteriorates, results become even less reliable. But a semaphore beacon could suffer significant deterioration, to perhaps half the brightness, and still be just as accurate in sending messages.

The disadvantage of a digital device, is that not as much information can be transmitted at once. An ordinary telephone handset receives sound as an analogue signal (the distortion of the diaphragm in the microphone is proportional to the frequency and loudness of your voice). And because of this you can transfer a lot of information quickly. If you were to communicate using morse code, you would first need to convert every letter of your message into code, and then send the message letter by letter: a much slower process.

If computers were built using analogue principles, the result of a numerical calculation could be represented by the voltage in a wire. An answer of 1, could be represented by one volt, two by two volts, and answers in between could be represented by fractions of a volt. But in a digital system, one wire has only two states: 'on' or 'off'. Therefore it can represent only two numbers '0' or '1'.

Electronic machines are susceptible to many influences such as changes in temperature and magnetic fields. Therefore the voltages passing through individual components can vary quite significantly with conditions. By requiring a wire to be in only one of two possible states, large margins of error are possible, and high degrees of accuracy are possible. (It is as if you used your bathroom scales to tell you only if you were standing on them or not).

In a computer, every operation is carried out using two indicators only. Instructions to the computer (computer programs) are represented by lists of '0's and '1's; Numbers are represented by lists of '0's and '1's; and Text is represented by lists of '0's and '1's. How is this done? Let's start by looking at Numbers.

Representing Numbers in Digital Systems

In our conventional numbering system, we count numbers in groups of ten. It is easy to see how our numbering system evolved in this way, we have ten fingers which form a convenient counting aid. But there is no reason why we cannot count in groups of five, seven, twelve, or any other number. We could even count in groups of two, using only the digits 0 and 1. In Figure 2.5, the first two columns show the numbers one to sixteen using the conventional (Decimal) system; the second column shows the same numbers using a system where only the figures 0 and 1 are used. This two digit system is called the Binary system.

Counting in the binary system follows the same rules as in our usual, decimal system. The count starts at '0', then '1'. But then you've run out of numbers, so just as you do when you get to 9 in the decimal system, you have to start a new column to the left at '10'. The next number is '11', but then you run out of numbers again, so you have to start a new column to the left at '100'. Following this pattern, you can continue forever. The only real problem is the amount of space needed. By the time you reach the equivalent of sixteen in the decimal system, you're into five figure numbers already. People working with computers use a shorthand way of representing binary numbers, using the **hexadecimal** system. (This is explained in Appendix A.)

All calculations done by computers are carried out working with binary numbers. And the only calculation that computers can carry out are to add, subtract, and compare binary numbers. All problems have to be reduced to these terms. Addition is done by converting numbers to binary numbers, adding them, and then converting back to decimal. Multiplication is done by repeated addition of binary numbers (for example, seven times eight is worked out by converting seven to the binary number 111, and then adding it to itself eight times). Similarly, division is done by repeated subtraction (to find out how many times seven goes into fifty-six, you keep taking seven away from fifty-six until you have nothing left - using binary numbers, of course). Even operations on text are carried out by reducing the problem to that of simple mathematics on binary numbers. This is why the binary system is so basic to computing.

The Binary system	
Decimal	Binary
1	0001
2	0010
3	0011
4	0100
5	0101
6	0110
7	0111
8	1000
9	1001
10	1010
11	1011
12	1100
13	1101
14	1110
15	1111
16	10000

Figure 2.5

But, happily, you do not *need* to know anything about the binary system in order to get full use out of a computer (no more than you need to know anything about transistors, or cathode ray tubes in order to enjoy a television programme). But life would lose its richness if you never explored unnecessary territory. So, if you are interested, there is a more detailed account of the binary system in Appendix A.

Representing Text in Digital Systems

If everything in a digital system is represented by two numbers, '0' and '1', and all computer operations must be in binary arithmetic, how do we represent text? Obviously some convention is needed, so that each letter is represented by a given group of '0's and '1's. It doesn't matter how this is done, as long as it is consistent. And every computer manufacturer could use a different convention if they so chose. But if every computer did use a different convention, it could lead to chaos in systems where different machines had to communicate with each other. So it is fortunate that the vast majority of computers use one of two conventions:

1.   EBCDIC (Extended Binary Coded Decimal Interchange Code)
2.   ASCII (American Standard Code for Information Interchange)

EBCDIC is used in IBM mainframe computers and their imitations. ASCII is used by nearly all other computers (including IBM PCs). So it is ASCII that will be used by your computer and it is ASCII that we shall deal with in this book.

Code in Binary	Code in Decimal	Character
0100001	33	!
0100010	34	"
0100011	35	#
0110001	49	1
0110010	50	2
1000001	65	A
1000010	66	B
1000011	67	C
1100001	97	a
1100010	98	b
1100011	99	c

Figure 2.6

In the ASCII system each letter is represented by a binary number 7 digits long. So the binary codes for text characters in the ASCII system range from 0000000 to 1111111. The decimal equivalent of

1111111 is 127, so one hundred and twenty seven characters can be represented in the ASCII system. Most of the characters represented are the usual textual characters; lower case a-z, upper case A-Z, numbers 0-9, other characters such as !"#$%'&*()-_+=?@. Figure 2.6 shows some example ASCII codes.

Not all ASCII codes represent printable characters. Why? Because some characters are reserved for special purposes. When a computer sends a text file to a printer, the computer will need to send certain instructions, such as when to start a new line, or when to feed in a new sheet of paper. And the printer might need to send instructions to the computer, telling it when it is ready to receive more text, or asking the computer to stop sending text until the printer catches up (the computer will be able to transmit the text a lot faster than the printer can print it). So some of the ASCII codes have been reserved for special instructions. For example the ASCII character with the binary code 00001101 is the Carriage Return character, which tells the printer to start a new line.

A listing of ASCII character codes is shown in Appendix A.

Earlier, we said that there were three things that we needed to represent in the computer:

1. Numbers
2. Text
3. Instructions that tell the computer what to do

We have covered how numbers and text are represented. But to understand how instructions are represented, you need to know how a computer works. We will cover this in the next section.

The Engine Room

Figure 2.7 is a representation of the nerve centre of a personal computer. The diagram looks complicated at first glance, but we will spend some time in explaining the diagram in detail.

The key element, the device that does most of the work, is the Central Processing Unit (CPU). The CPU is a silicon chip impregnated with a number of electronic devices. The rest of the machine is dedicated to co-ordinating the intricate choreography of feeding information to the CPU as it is required, and taking away the results of work done.

The CPU carries out its functions by manipulating the information held in its **registers**. In Figure 2.7 the registers are represented by the rectangles marked A, F, B, C, D, E, H, L, IX, IY. Because computers

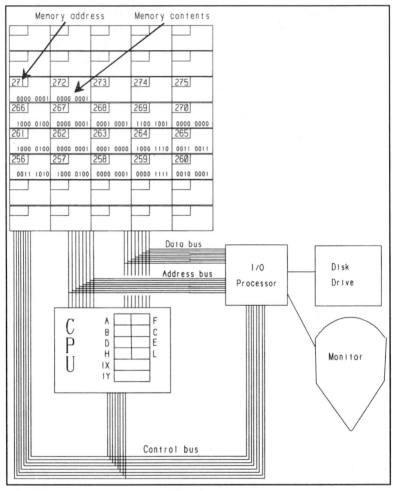

Figure 2.7

are digital devices, the information stored in each part of the register can only be in one of two states, 'off' or 'on', which can otherwise be represented as '0' or '1'. In practice this is achieved by either the absence or the presence of a voltage in a minute electronic component (over 1 million such components can be held in a device the size of a postage stamp).

In the chip that we have chosen for our example, the Z80 chip (very old fashioned by today's standards, but suitable for our purposes), each register can hold eight bits of information. Thus the contents of a register may be represented as a binary number; for example: 0010 1101. Each item of information (i.e. each '0' or '1') is referred to as a Bit. A group of eight bits is called a Byte.

The CPU is able to carry out certain operations on the information held in its registers. For example, we could tell the CPU to set the A register to a given binary number. Or we could ask the CPU to add 1 to the number in the A register. Or we could move the number in the C register to the A register. Simple arithmetic is possible; we can tell the CPU to add the number in the D register to the A register.

How do we tell the CPU what instructions to carry out? The instructions are held in **Memory**. Sometimes memory is referred to as RAM (Random Access Memory).

The computers memory is organized like a box of pigeon holes. Each pigeon hole has a label, or **Memory Address**. Memory addresses are numbers allocated sequentially. So the first memory address is 0, the second 1, etc. up to the limit of addressable memory (which will depend on the design of the machine).

When the computer is instructed to run a program, the program is copied from the Disk where it is stored into memory. In Figure 2.7, a program has been copied into memory, and occupies space starting at memory address 256.

Once the program has been copied into memory, the CPU will start to execute the program. The first byte of the program is copied from memory and transferred to the CPU. Because there are eight bits in a byte, eight wires are needed to transfer one byte of information simultaneously. This pathway of parallel wires is called a Bus. The first byte of memory is passed down the Data Bus to the CPU. The CPU knows that this first byte of the program is an instruction.

The instruction will tell the CPU to do something with its registers. For example, it might tell the CPU to add the number in the C register to the number in the A register. Each make of computer chip has a standard set of instructions which it can carry out, this is often referred to as the chip's **instruction set**.

Some instructions will tell the CPU to set a register to a particular number, or get a number from a specified location in memory. Because these instructions need to pass data to the CPU (the number to go in the register, or the memory address to access) they will take up more space than other instructions. For example, in Figure 2.7, the instruction at memory address 256, '0011 1010', asks the computer to load the A register with the number which can be found in the memory address given by the two bytes following. One byte for the instruction, and two bytes for the memory address. The two bytes following give the binary number '0000 0001 0001 0000', this converts to 272 in decimal, so the computer will then load the number at memory address 272 into the A register (look at Figure 2.7, and you will see that the number at memory address 272 is '0000 0001'; this is the number that will be put into the A register). Because the chip knows that the previous instruction has used up three bytes (or three memory pigeon holes), it now looks at memory address 259 for its next instruction. This process carries on until execution of the program is completed. The chip always knows where to look for its next instruction because it counts how many bytes the previous instruction used, and moves on to the next available memory location. This is how the computer is able to separate *instructions* from *data* (numbers or text). The program shown in Figure 2.7 accomplishes the task of adding together one and one. If your are interested, the program is explained in greater depth in Appendix B.

The CPU is the engine of the machine. It can add things together, move them around and carry out all the necessary tasks. The memory of the computer, is the scratch pad. It is used for two purposes:

1. To hold the list of instructions for the CPU to carry out.
2. To act as a work sheet, which the CPU can use to store numbers, and place the results of work done.

In the example program we have just looked at, the only interaction that has taken place has been between the CPU and the computer's memory. But the CPU can do more than this. It can copy data from disk into memory, and copy the results of work done from the memory back onto disk. The CPU can also send the contents of memory to the monitor, or indeed to any other output device that may be connected to the computer, such as a printer.

Up until now we have been careful to make the distinction between, Instructions, Numbers, and Characters. But it is important to realize that this is only a distinction to suit our convenience.

As far as the computer is concerned, the distinction is between **instructions** and **operands**. When you instruct the computer to place a binary number at a memory address, it is of no consequence to the machine whether you eventually wish to use it as a number or a character. The distinction is entirely in the mind of the user. As far as the CPU is concerned a byte of code is either something telling it what to do (an Instruction) or a piece of data that has to be processed (an operand).

To display a group of characters on the screen, you first store in memory the ASCII codes for the characters you wish to display. Then tell the CPU to send these codes to the monitor. The monitor expects to receive ASCII characters and interprets them accordingly. Similarly, when data is sent to the printer, it expects to receive ASCII characters. As far as the CPU is concerned it is just shovelling binary numbers around. It is the output device, the monitor or printer, which recognizes the ASCII convention and interprets characters accordingly.

It is worth remembering that without devices to collect and input data and display results a computer would be useless. For example, the program that we used to illustrate how the CPU works is completely useless. Why? Because the user can not see what the computer is doing, and has no way of finding out the results of the work done. Input and Output devices are collectively known as Peripherals. There are many sorts of devices that can be attached to a computer to greatly enhance the effectiveness of the machine. We will take a detailed look at these in Chapter 5.

Our detailed look at the heart of the machine, must paint a very unfriendly picture of computers. All the instructions are represented by scores of '0's and '1's. And so many '0's and '1's for such a simple program. How do the instructions get there? Does the person who writes the instructions (the programmer) type in the '0's and '1's?

Fortunately, things are a lot easier than that. Of course from your point of view, you may not care how the programmer gets the instructions into the machine as the eventual system is easy for you to use. But it is instructive to see how it is done.

Producing a Computer Program

You now know what a computer program looks like at its lowest level. It is simply a long string of '0's and '1's, broken down into byte-sized chunks and copied into the memory of the machine.

You also know that each byte of code represents either an instruction or an operand.

But a programmer does not have to enter these codes by hand. The programmer writes a list of commands in a special form, known as a programming language. The programmer then uses another program to turn these commands into the list of '0's and '1's that the machine will recognize. The program in its final form (i.e. '0's and '1's) is called **machine code**.

In the past, programming languages fell into two categories: **low-level** languages and **high-level** languages. Low-level languages provide commands that correspond directly to the functions that the CPU is able to carry out. High-level languages are generally easier to use and give the programmer much greater freedom to specify complex instructions and conditions. Today, languages are available which are even easier to use than high-level languages; these are known as **fourth generation** languages. In a fourth generation language instructions are similar to everyday English. Fourth generation languages can be picked up quickly and used by people with no programming experience. And development doesn't stop there! There are Fifth generation languages becoming available which are said to be even easier to use than fourth generation languages. But let's start at the bottom, by looking at low-level languages.

Low-level languages

On most machines, there is only one low-level language - Assembler. An assembler instruction (called a mnemonic) corresponds exactly with a machine code instruction.

The example program that we used in Figure 2.7 could be written in assembler as follows:

Binary Code	Assembler	Description
0011 1010	LD A, (0110)	Load A register with number at address 110h (in assembler
0000 0001		numbers are expressed in
0001 0000		*hexadecimal* - covered in Appendix A).
0010 0001	LD HL, 0111	Load HL registers with number
0000 0001		0111h
0001 0001		
1000 1110	ADD A, (HL)	Add the contents of address given by HL registers to the A register
0011 0010	LD (0112), A	Put the contents of the A
0000 0001		register at memory address 112h
0001 0010		
1100 1001	RET	Finish.

This example is intended to show you what assembler looks like, there is no need to study it in detail.

To create a file of assembler code, the programmer will use a program called a **file editor**. A file editor allows you to type in characters, line by line at the terminal, and then look at, and amend what you have typed in. The file editor will write the result onto disk as an ASCII file (so the file can be displayed on the monitor or sent to the printer). To produce a machine code program from the ASCII file of assembler code the programmer uses another program called an **assembler**. The assembler reads the file of assembler instructions and interprets them to produce a file containing the program, i.e. a file of machine code. (In practice an intermediate stage, called *linking* takes place, but, essentially, this is just an extension of the assembly process.)

So much for the technicalities, what can we say about assembler as a programming language? As you can see from the listing, assembler is a great improvement on using binary code, but it is still a cumbersome series of steps to achieve our objective of adding one plus one! Is there an alternative? Yes. We can use a high-level language.

High-level Languages

A high-level language allows you to use a much wider and more powerful list of instructions to produce a program. There are many high-level languages. Some of these languages are more suited to some purposes than others. For example, one language might have facilities which make it easier to manipulate text, while another might have powerful mathematical facilities. A programmer might use the first language to produce a word-processor, but chose the second to develop a statistical package.

As an example of how much easier it is to use a high-level language, consider the example program we used to add one plus one. In BASIC (a program language commonly used by beginners), this could be achieved using the statement:

X = 1 + 1

Also, the program could be improved immeasurably by adding the line:

PRINT "The result of 1 + 1 is "; X

This second statement will cause the machine to display the result of the calculation on the monitor. The wider range of facilities, conciseness of expression and ease of use means that programmers can write programs much more easily and quickly using a high-level language than they can with assembler.

How does a programmer use a high-level language? The process is very similar to using Assembler. The programmer uses a file editor to enter the listing in the high-level language and a program called a Compiler to produce the program (as with assembler a linking stage is necessary to produce the final code).

If high-level languages are so good, why should anyone ever need to use assembler? When the compiler translates a high-level language instruction into machine code, it will produce many machine code instructions for each high-level language instruction. It may be possible for a skilled assembler programmer to produce the same result using fewer instructions by writing the code in assembler. So, assembler is used to produce programs where speed of execution is important (many computer games are written in assembler). Another reason why a programmer may wish to use assembler is to make use of special features of a particular piece of hardware. For example, the way in which one type of computer is built, may differ from another, even though they are based around the same type of chip. Because of this, the way in which the chip controls the monitor, or disk drive, might vary between one computer and another. A clever programmer may make use of these differences to enhance the performance of a program on a particular machine. To do this, he will need to write in assembler to directly control how the chip operates.

We have been looking at the heart of the machine and the production of programs in some detail. But there are still some considerable gaps in our knowledge. For example, we know what a program is and how it is produced, but how do we start it running? And if we have several programs stored on one disk, how do we find out what they are? And if we wanted to move a program from one disk to another, how could we go about it? The CPU only understands one language: Do we have to send instructions in machine code?

Fortunately, we do not have to communicate directly with the CPU. In most cases the user can achieve what needs to be done by typing in simple commands at the terminal. How is this possible? Because there is a special program which is always running which makes the bridge between the user and the CPU. This special program is called the Operating System.

The Operating System

For a computer to be of use, it must satisfy certain requirements.

From the user's point of view, there must be an easy way to carry out basic tasks, such as run programs, copy files from one disk to another, or look at what programs are stored on a disk.

From the programmer's point of view, it should be possible to write a program that uses devices such as disks, monitors and printers without having a detailed engineering knowledge of the way the machine was built.

There must be an *interface* between the user and the machine. This interface is called the **Operating System**. We will look at how this interface works from two points of view. First, from the user's point of view; then from the programmers point of view.

The Operating System and the User

After switching the computer on, the first step is to load the operating system into the machine's memory. How this is done will depend on the set-up of your machine. If you do not have a hard disk, you will put a floppy disk containing the operating system program into the disk drive. This floppy disk is usually called a **system disk.** If your machine has a hard disk, it is usual for a copy of the operating system program to be kept on it. Some home computers store the operating system in a special kind of memory which retains information when the machine is switched off. But wherever your operating system program is stored, the first thing our computer will do is look for it and load it into memory. When the operating system program is in memory, it will run and take control of the machine.

The operating system program creates an environment enabling the user to carry out basic tasks. The way that this is done will depend on the machine. There are two common methods. Some modern computers, such as the Apple Macintosh, present the user with a screen full of pictures representing the available options. The user operates a device called a Mouse which rolls around on the desk. As the mouse moves, so does an arrow on the screen. When the arrow points to the picture representing the desired option, the user clicks a button on the mouse and the operation is carried out. This type of interface is easy to learn and especially popular with people who are wary of the technical aspects of computers. This type of user interface is often called a **WIMP** (Windows Icons Menus and Pointers).

The other type of operating environment uses a more traditional approach. The user types in commands at the terminal and the system responds accordingly. For example, to see all the files held on your disk, you would normally type 'dir' (for directory) and the system would produce a list of file names on the monitor. The two dominant operating systems in this area are CP/M (used on older business machines and the Amstrad PCW range) and DOS (used on IBM PCs and compatibles). Because of the popularity of the WIMP system used on the Macintosh, there are several programs on offer to create a similar environment for other machines, notably Digital Research's GEM program, which Amstrad supplies as standard with its range of IBM compatible PCs, and Microsoft's Windows program (both covered in Chapter 4). IBM's latest operating system, OS/2, utilizes a WIMP type interface.

For the purposes of our examples, we will assume that we are working with the DOS operating system, as it is the most commonly used in practice. When the computer is idle, waiting for a command, it shows a prompt in the form:

A>

The first letter denotes which disk drive you are currently using. Disk drives are denoted by letters. Floppy disk drives are normally called A and B, a hard disk drive is normally called C. So, if you were using a machine with a hard disk, and you were using the C drive, the prompt would show:

C>

You can switch to using a different disk drive at any time by entering the drive letter followed by a colon. For example, to switch from the C drive to the A drive you would enter A:

Handling Files and Running Programs

Files held on disk normally have a two-part name of the form D:filename.ext where D: denotes which disk drive the file is on, filename is a name of up to eight characters long and ext is an extension of up to three characters long. The file extension can be used to indicate what type of data the file contains. Programs are normally held in files with an extension of COM or EXE. For example, the Wordstar program is normally held in a file called WS.COM. To run a program you type in the first part of the filename, so to run the Wordstar program, you would type in 'ws'.

Files may be erased, renamed or copied to another disk drive by entering commands at the keyboard. For example, if you were using the C drive and you wished to copy the wordstar program file to the A drive you would enter the command:

C> copy ws.com a:

If you were using a WIMP type environment operating system to copy one file from one drive to another, you would use the mouse to point at the file, click the button, and simply drag the file's icon (screen image representing the file) from one disk icon to another.

So that's how the operating system makes life easier for the user. But what does it do for the programmer?

The Operating System and the Programmer

There are many different types of computers in the world, using a variety of construction techniques. If you examined computers by ten different manufacturers, you might find ten different systems used for such things as controlling the screen output, accessing the disk drives, communicating with the printer. This situation is a potential nightmare for the programmer. For every computer system, he would have to write a separate program to take account of the machine's peculiarities. And he would not be able to write in a high-level language. Because controlling physical devices is done on a low level, by the chip (there is usually a separate purpose-built chip working in tandem with the CPU dedicated solely to handling input and output devices). In practice this is not a problem. Why? Because the operating system provides a consistent interface between the programmer and the hardware.

The consequence of this is that any program written for the operating system on one computer, should also work on another computer using the same operating system. When programmers write programs (generically called software) they do not write for a particular machine, they write for a particular Operating System. This has other advantages. For example the Commodore Amiga and Acorn Archimedes computers both use their own operating systems. But both are also able to emulate the DOS operating system used on IBM PCs. So these computers cannot only use the software written for them, but can also run programs written for the IBM PC.

Sometimes, a computer running an operating system originally designed for another machine is unable to behave in an exactly similar fashion. So that while, for example, most programs would run satisfactorily, in some cases programs would crash (or, fall over - technical terms for cease to work!). When a computer is described as 100% compatible with another computer, this means that it will run all programs written for the other computer.

When we looked at our example program, earlier on in the chapter, we said that the computer copies the program into memory and then executes each instruction one byte at a time. How does the computer run the operating system program and the user's program (sometimes called an application program)? Consider the diagram in Figure 2.8.

The figure shows the way memory is used under the CP/M operating system. Memory addresses up to 100h are taken up by the operating system (100h is the hexadecimal number equivalent to 256 in decimal). Also, memory addresses at the top of memory are taken up by the operating system. The remaining memory is available for application programs ('normal' programs are often called application programs, to distinguish them from the operating system program). When the computer is 'idle' it is running the operating system program. When the operating system program determines that the user wants to run an application program (because you have typed in the name of a program) it copies the program into the Transient Program Area of memory (TPA). The TPA starts at memory address 100h. The computer then starts reading instructions at memory address 100h, so the application program has control. The CPU will execute each instruction, one byte at a time as we described above. When the program wishes to carry out a machine dependent task (i.e. an instruction that is non-standard from one computer to the next) it will pass control to the operating system. When the task is complete, control will be passed back to the application program. This is how an operating system provides a consistent environment.

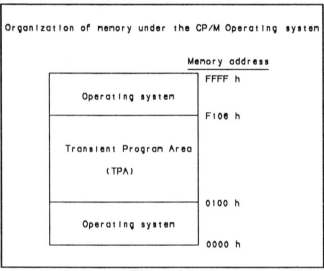

Figure 2.8

For example, in the CP/M operating system if you wish to display a string of characters on the monitor (for example, a sentence), you proceed as follows:

1. Place the string terminated by a $ character (in ASCII form) somewhere in memory.
2. Put the number 9 in the C register of the CPU.
3. Put the memory address where the string is stored in the D and E registers of the CPU (two registers are required as a memory address takes up two bytes, and a register has only one byte).
4. Tell the CPU to start executing instructions from memory location 0005h.

Memory location 0005h is in that part of memory occupied by the operating system. So it is the operating system program that actually does the work of displaying the string. When the operating system has finished doing this, it will automatically pass control back to the application program. Later, when the application program wishes to do other machine specific tasks it will again call on the operating system to do so.

We have completed our journey through the technical intricacies of the computer. We shall lean heavily on what we have learnt when we look at choosing hardware, in Chapter 5. In the next Chapter we return to more familiar territory. We shall show you how to look at your business, and come up with a definitive statement of your processing needs. But first let's summarize what we have done in this Chapter.

Summary of Chapter Two - What is a Computer?

At the beginning of the Chapter we looked at the main components of a Personal Computer: the System Unit, the Monitor, and the Keyboard. We learnt that computers read sets of instructions from programs which are stored as files held on disks.

When a user runs a program, communication is interactive. The user types commands at the keyboard and reads the response of the machine on the monitor screen.

We looked at the distinction between analogue and digital systems. In a digital system a source of information can have only two states 'on' or 'off' like an electric light. These states are commonly represented by '0' and '1'. In an analogue system the information conveyed by a source is proportionate in some way to something else - such as a set of bathroom scales where the distance moved by the scale is proportionate to your weight.

Analogue systems can be unreliable. Consequently most computers are digital machines, and nearly all information: numbers, text, machine instructions is stored as a sequence of '0's and '1's.

We saw how numbers can be represented using the binary system.

Text characters are represented using the ASCII convention. This convention is relevant to output devices, rather than to the computer itself. A printer or monitor will interpret any signal sent to it as if it were an ASCII signal. The engine of the computer, the CPU, regards everything as either an instruction or an operand.

The CPU reads instructions from memory, and processes information in byte sized chunks of eight bits at a time. A bit is an individual '0' or '1'. The CPU manipulates the bytes held in its registers according to the instructions it reads from memory. The CPU can also use the memory as a scratch pad to store the results of its calculations. It can then copy information in memory on to disk or send it to the monitor or printer.

Computer programs are produced by programmers in low-level languages and high-level languages. In a low-level language, such as assembler, each instruction corresponds to a machine code instruction. In a high-level language, such as BASIC, powerful instructions are provided which may correspond to many machine code instructions. A program is assembled (if it is an assembler program) or compiled (if it is written in a high-level language) to produce a file containing the final program.

The interface between the user and the machine is provided by a special program, called the operating system. The operating system provides the user with a number of convenient facilities: being able to run programs, looking at what files are held on disk, copying files from one disk to another, erasing files.

The operating system provides the programmer with a consistent interface to the machine's hardware, so that programs can be written using devices such as the monitor and printer without the programmer needing to know specific information about the way in which the machine is constructed. Programs are therefore written for Operating Systems, and not for specific machines.

Modern Operating systems are designed to work with a hand-held mouse device moving a pointer against pictures on a screen, to make it easier for non-technical people to use computers.

CHAPTER 3

Assessing Your Needs

In the first chapter, we looked at how a computer can help you control your paperwork. We saw how the three main activities in a typical office (correspondence, filing, and accounts) can be made easier by using programs called Word Processors, Databases, and Spreadsheets.

We then took some time in Chapter 2 to take a detailed look at how computers work. So now you know what a computer is, and how it can be used. Why not go out, buy a machine, pick up a Word Processor, Database, and a Spreadsheet program and all your problems will be solved?

Many people do just that. Some do it without even knowing the basic things that you have discovered in the first two chapters of this book. And therein lies the cause of many disasters. It is most unlikely that simply buying three packages is the best course for you to follow; there will be no integration between the new packages and your current system. And there will probably be very little common ground between the packages themselves. For a system to function efficiently, it must work as a single cohesive unit. When you introduce a computer, it is important that tasks taken over by the computer link seamlessly with the parts of the system that will continue to function manually. Many newcomers to computing make the mistake of seeing the computer as the 'solution'. This is a fundamental mistake. It is the system design that provides the solution. A computer is only a tool that may make it possible to implement some parts of the system efficiently.

There is absolutely no point in buying a computer until you have produced a complete, precise description of how you want to use it.

There are two words worth emphasizing: *complete*, and *precise*.

Why complete? Let's take an example. Once you see how useful a word processor could be in helping control your correspondence, you may be tempted to rush out and buy a computer for word processing.

It may be expensive, but if you intend to transfer your filing, accounts and stock control systems onto the same computer at a later date, the cost would be justified. But what if the computer you buy isn't suitable for your other systems? Your hasty decision now becomes doubly expensive because you have to buy two computers instead of one.

And why must you have a precise description of what you intend to computerize? Implementing a computer system is not a straightforward process. These days, the cost of the hardware is deceptively cheap. However, the major costs of implementing a computer system are not hardware costs, but costs of disruption, implementation and training. It is quite common for a business to incur large amounts of unexpected expense in implementing a system. Sometimes the costs are much higher than they should be, because the system chosen is not suitable for the needs of the business; much of the effort goes into 'bending' and 'tweaking' the system to try and meet the business needs. And sometimes, after vast sums have been spent in trying to 'bend' a system unsuccessfully, the whole cost of computerization has to be written off.

The only way you can hope to avoid these pitfalls, is to have a precise, complete description of what your real needs are. Many businessmen are convinced that they have this sort of understanding. But often, when it comes to drawing out a detailed specification for a system, it transpires that many of the needs perceived by businessmen are not real, but merely symptoms of underlying causes hiding a deeper need.

In this chapter you will find out how to look at your business objectively. You will learn how to analyse the way your business operates, and build up a description of your needs that will form the foundation stone for your eventual, efficient system.

To achieve a deep understanding of how your business works, you must look at it in two different ways:

1. What are the underlying needs of the business?
2. How does the business operate *as a system*?

Every business can be looked at as a system, because every business receives input, processes it, and produces output. Many of the terms used in the computer world reflect this 'processing of information' point of view. Computer applications are often referred to as DP (Data Processing), EDP (Electronic Data Processing), or the more fashionable IT (Information Technology).

This technique of looking at a business as a system is used by all major companies and public bodies developing computer applications. The considerations are the same, whether you are implementing a multi-million dollar application, or an inexpensive system for a small business. The only difference is that a large installation will have many staff devoted to systems development and there is a distinct separation of responsibilities. Let's take some time to look at how a large company produces a computer system. Many of the techniques used are just as valid for implementing even the smallest systems.

Staff in a commercial DP department will normally fall into the following categories: Project leaders, Business analysts, System analysts, Programmers, and Operational staff.

Project leaders co-ordinate the development of a system, directing staff, commissioning resources, resolving problems, and generally taking care of all the things that need to be done for the system to be ready on time.

Business analysts look at the business needs of the organization. On a given project they will be responsible for producing a document that states exactly what needs to happen for the business to function efficiently. This document will list what information is being received, what form it is in (e.g. letters, invoices, remittance advices), what processing needs to be done, and what output must be produced (e.g. management reports, accounting statements, invoices, cheques). The business analyst's report will include explanatory diagrams and will probably have flowcharts showing how information flows through the business and what processing is carried out.

Once an analysis of business needs has been carried out, two documents need to be produced: a Functional Specification, and a Technical Specification.

A functional specification describes what the proposed system will do from the user's point of view. (Computer people call anybody who uses a computer system a 'user'. Usually, users are not computer people). Examples of all screen layouts, forms and reports will be included, together with a general description of the processing to be carried out. The functional specification will probably be written by the business analyst.

But sometimes, the functional specification will be written by the **systems analyst** who, in any event, will write the technical specification. The technical specification contains a complete description of the proposed system in technical terms. It will describe what hardware the system will run on (usually the on-site mainframe will be assumed), how processes are to be carried out, what kind of storage devices are used to hold information (usually disks, but on a big system these will always be hard disks with a much greater capacity than the hard disk on a PC), and how the files holding the information on the computer will be organized. The technical specification will certainly contain many detailed flowcharts. It acts as a design template for building the system.

Under the direction of the project leader, **programmers** work from the technical specification to produce the code for the system. Computer facilities are provided and maintained by **operational staff.**

So, in very general terms, that's how a big company develops an application. The main steps can be summarized as follows:

1. Construct a logical model of the business (equivalent to the business analyst's report and the functional specification).
2. Construct a physical model that shows how the logical model can be implemented practically.
3. Acquire the hardware (if necessary).
4. Acquire the software (either by writing programs or buying a package).
5. Implement the system.

The main difference between implementing a system for a small business and a large business is that with a large business the software will usually be written rather than bought, whereas a small business is likely to choose an off-the-shelf package. Buying packaged software is often highly cost effective, especially if the features offered by the package represent a close match to the needs of the business. Disadvantages of packages are that they inevitably introduce some measure of compromise, and you are stuck with the system you buy. You cannot alter commercial software because it is *compiled* code (see Chapter 2). With software written to order the source code can be altered to add new features and re-compiled.

The main advantage of using software written to order is that you can specify precisely what the system should do. The biggest disadvantage is the considerable cost, especially in comparison with the falling cost of packaged software. However, with the advent of fourth generation languages (4GLs) the process of producing an application has been made considerably easier and cheaper.

If it seems likely that a business is going to end up by compromising and buying an off-the-shelf package, why waste time defining business needs? What is the point of working out exactly what you need, only to find that it isn't available?

It is precisely because of the limitations imposed by packaged software that the process of understanding the business needs and specifying requirements is so important. Already, the small businessman is likely to be working to a compromise: ill defined requirements can lead to a poor choice of software that fails to meet business needs in crucial areas. And it is only by specifying requirements precisely that you can make the choice between proprietary software or a tailor-made solution.

Another area where the small-business is likely to differ from the large business is in choice of hardware. A large business will usually be constrained to use its established mainframe computer. A small businessman will often be setting up a system from scratch, and will have a free choice of hardware. There are two main considerations in choosing hardware:

1. Does it run the software that you need?
2. Does it have the storage capacity and processing speed that you require?

You will be able to answer this second question only when you have a precise definition of your business needs. We will look at this question at the end of this chapter, and again in Chapter 5.

The methods that you adopt to specify your requirements will be similar in many respects to the methods used by large businesses. The first step: building a logical model of the business, is equally important.

We will build a logical model of the business in five separate stages.

1. We will develop a list of the basic needs of the business. What is the business trying to achieve? What functions must the business carry out to meet these needs?
2. Next, we will start to build a picture of the business as a system. What information flows into the business, and what flows out?
3. Then, we will categorize business information, and establish what volumes we have to deal with.
4. Next, we will complete our picture of the business-system by determining what processes are carried out and how the system fits together.
5. Finally, we will use our model of the business to determine whether a PC based solution is feasible, and if not, what hardware category should be considered.

The first step, then, is to list your basic needs.

Establishing Basic Needs

Your list of needs forms the criteria for judging your proposed system. As you specify the system you will return to this list to ascertain whether the system meets your needs. If the list of needs is wrong, everything will be wrong.

How can a businessman not know what his needs are? Usually because familiarity with a certain way of doing things can fool a person into thinking that it is the procedure that is important, and not the original reason for instigating the procedure. Let's take an example.

You are a systems analyst investigating a business with the purpose of drawing up a plan for computerization. You start off by asking the owner: What do you need out of the system? What must it do?

The following two items appear on the owner's list:

1. Goods received notes must be filed by supplier.
2. The cash book must be laid out with separate analysis columns.

Now, you could design your system so that it conforms to these requests, or you could look deeper, and ask the owner: Why should it be like this? After a moment's thought the owner might respond:

1. The goods received notes must be in supplier order because I sometimes need to check whether the goods have been delivered before I pay a supplier's invoice.
2. At the end of the week I like to be able to see what I've spent money on. By keeping separate columns in the cash book, I can look at the running totals and see at a glance where the money has gone.

So, the original items on the list were not needs at all. The corresponding real needs of the business are:

1. To ensure that money is paid out only when goods have been received and checked.
2. To keep a close scrutiny on cash balances and spending patterns.

In a computer system both of these needs might be catered for in a far more efficient way than the methods currently used.

The requirement to check invoices would not exist if the system processed payments automatically, checking details of goods received against both the delivery notes and purchase orders before allowing a payment to be made. Furthermore, the system might be set up to release payments only when the full period of credit has been taken; a considerable improvement on the present method. With a new system in action, the tedious and time consuming job of sorting and filing goods received notes could be dispensed with. They could be batched up and filed by day of receipt as soon as the details are entered into the computer.

With a fully automated payments system, the requirement for a cash book with analysis columns might also disappear. The computer could produce a regular, detailed summary of cash balances and disbursements.

Many businesses under-utilize computers because they haven't produced a complete description of their needs. In the example above, the owner of the business had come to accept that only a certain amount was possible under the old system, and he thought in terms of that system. Under a manual system a full blown credit control system was impractical, and a payments analysis was confined to the columns that were available in the cash book. With a computer system, control can be exercised much more effectively. But this can not be achieved if the need is not recognized. When the need is recognized, it is possible to assess whether a computer solution is feasible.

How can you get to the real needs of the business? The first stage is to make out a list of high-level needs. These needs should state your *primary business objectives*, and *encapsulate the essence of your business philosophy*. Let's take an example.

We will use an imaginary company throughout the rest of this book, and follow through a computer system installation from start to finish. The example company provides interior design consultancy. The company has seven staff, four designers, an office administrator, a secretary, and a general manager. At present the company uses no computers. The secretary uses an electric typewriter, the administrator uses a manual bookkeeping and filing system. The designers produce promotional schematics and detailed designs by hand. The main business of the company is re-design and refurbishment of property interiors. All building and decorating work is supervised by a designer, and carried out by a company-approved sub-contractor.

We will use the example company to develop a list of needs and produce a logical model of the business in this chapter. When we look at designing and implementing the system in Chapters 6 and 7, we will return again to the example company and build on the work that we start here.

The general manger's priorities are:

Profitability
Strong cash levels
High quality finished product
Materials always available
Outstanding customer service

The philosophy behind the business is to sell a high value, quality product at the top end of the market. The list of priorities reflects this.

There may be some conflict within your list; for example, 'Profitability', 'Strong cash levels' and 'Materials always available' do not always go together: profitability is achieved by expansion, which eats up cash. On the other hand, if you want to hold your assets as stock, you can't hold your assets as cash at the same time. But nevertheless, these are all valid objectives, which need not always operate at the expense of one another. Indeed, if you intend to finance

expansion and a high stock value at the same time it is important that
you do aim for strong cash levels by any other means available to you.

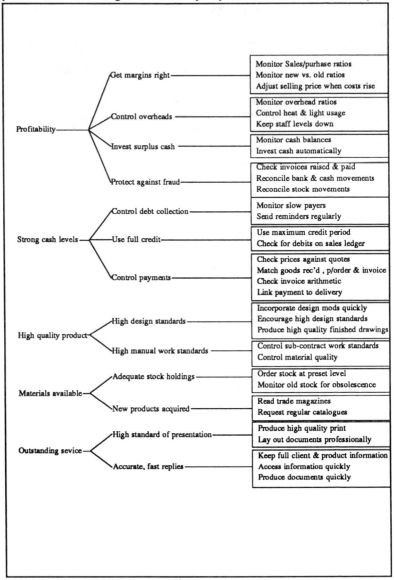

Figure 3.1

Once you have set your primary objectives, make a list of all your subsidiary business needs. By successively breaking down the needs on your high-level list, you will eventually get to the stage where you can list what functions the business must carry out at a low level. An example breakdown for the interior design company is shown in Figure 3.1. (This example has been taken to a level of detail where it is useful as an instrument of instruction. In practice, a much longer list may result.)

When you break down your business objectives, concentrate on functions rather than procedures. It is important to list what you want done rather than how it is achieved. Don't constrain yourself by what you think is possible; list what you'd like to be able to do. Be creative.

It isn't easy to think like this. You have too much knowledge and experience. You are used to the practicalities of living within routine constraints. But with a computer many of the constraints disappear. And one bright idea can transform your business.

Involve your staff right from the start. Their co-operation and enthusiasm will be essential if your eventual system is to work properly. Find out what they want from the system, and include it in your list of needs. Staff will be much more ready to accept a new way of working if they see benefits for them; and their attitude to work will change if they are consulted and respected for their opinion. At each stage in the process of system development, you should inform your staff of progress, and elicit their opinions when decisions have to be taken. Often, someone used to dealing with the day to day practicalities of a business is indispensable in differentiating between a good idea in theory, and workable proposition in practice.

When you compile your list of needs, forget about computers. If you anticipate what you intend to computerize, you will make a list to fit your preconceptions. Broaden your viewpoint: list everything you would like to do if you were completely unconstrained. In the list shown in Figure 3.1, some of the functions, such as 'read trade magazines', are far removed from computer operations. But it is the principle that is important. By forming a complete list of business functions you are less likely to overlook an opportunity.

Using a computer to replace an existing manual system often brings a great improvement to the running of a business. But the true potential of computers is realized only when you have the vision to use computers in new ways, and achieve things that were impossible before. In order to see these opportunities you must look at your business afresh. And that is why it is so important for you to make a complete list of functions when you analyse your business needs.

The detailed contents of the list will be affected by what priorities are set at the top. In the example, choosing 'Outstanding service' as a high business priority has resulted in an unusual amount of emphasis being placed on the functions 'Produce high quality print' and 'Lay out documents professionally'. But for a design consultancy serving an upper class market, presenting the right sort of image is crucial to success. If you have a strategy, make sure that it is reflected in your list of primary objectives. A strategy at the top is of no use unless it permeates throughout your business activities. By breaking down your business objectives from your strategic aims this permeation will occur as a matter of course.

Another point to notice about the example in Figure 3.1, is that the exercise of breaking down the business is by no means a trivial exercise. In order to list out functions that support the objective 'Protect against fraud', you have to know about techniques such as bank reconciliations and stock reconciliations. In order to carry out this exercise effectively, you must have a deep knowledge of your business and be aware of all the techniques available to you.

A computer cannot transform a bad businessman into a good businessman. If you don't know what you need to achieve, a computer cannot help you achieve it.

This fact is demonstrated time and time again in large organizations attempting to build computer applications. Often, the business analysts and system analysts engaged to work on a project have a strong background in DP, but a limited knowledge of the business. Specifications produced by analysts regurgitate the jargon used by the business experts, who consequently agree with the specification. But the analysts have no real understanding of the words they use. And it is only when the software is implemented that the end users find out that it does not meet their needs. The most successful companies employ people with a good understanding of the business to supervise the development of computer applications.

Once you have produced your list of business needs, the next step is to decide the best way to satisfy these needs. When we looked at the way a big company develops a system, we saw that specifying the mechanics of the system was a two stage process. First a logical model of the system was developed, then a physical model.

The logical model shows what information is held in the system, and the processing that is carried out. The logical model does not show what media the information is stored on (whether it is on paper or computer disks) or how the processing is achieved (whether it is carried out by a person or a computer). The logical model of your business will be equally valid whether you eventually decide to use a computer or not.

Once you have created a logical model you will have a complete description of your system requirements. You will then be able to review your logical model, decide how each process should be achieved, and thus create your physical model: a complete technical specification of the system. But you will not be able to do this until you have a much greater knowledge of the software and hardware that is available. For the remainder of this chapter, we will complete the stages of constructing a logical model. In the next two chapters we will look at software and hardware, and in Chapter 6 we will see how a physical model can be constructed.

You need a model showing how the business should operate. You will already know how the business currently operates. And there is a great temptation to build your model by simply repeating what you know about existing procedures. But if you follow this course there is a great danger that you will miss out on the available opportunities. It is better to pretend that you know nothing of the present system, and build your logical model from scratch. (Some consultants might dispute this, maintaining that a reliable, working manual system is the best foundation for a computer system. But this approach is sadly lacking in vision. Computers provide benefits not possible with manual systems. And system design should not be constrained by the limitations of manual systems. What *is* true, is that if you computerize a manual system that doesn't work, you will get a computer system that doesn't work.) By starting with a clean sheet, you can develop the best possible system to meet your needs.

The construction of your logical model should be driven by your list of needs. This may seem an obvious statement, but it is all too easy to produce your list of functions, and then forget about it, ploughing on to produce a model as if it was a completely separate exercise. Look at your list of needs and think hard about them before you start the modelling process.

As with listing of needs, there is no set way to build a logical model of the business. Most firms of consultants have their own standard approach (often, rather pretentiously referred to as a methodology). We will use a method that combines the best features of most systems, and is suitable for a small business.

Once you know what the needs of the business are, it is time to start looking at the business as a system. And the first questions to ask about a system are; What goes in? and What comes out?

Inputs and Outputs

Any system can be represented by the diagram in Figure 3.2

Figure 3.2

What are the most important things in the system shown in Figure 3.2? The Input and the Output. Why? Because if the input and the output are correct it doesn't matter how the system works or what processes are involved. It is the end result that matters.

Because of this, it is natural that you should start designing your business model by looking at Input and Output.

To give you a better idea of what we mean by input and output, let's look at a few practical examples.

Often, most of the input to the system will be pre-determined. For example, in many businesses three main sources of input are:

1. Cheques and remittance advices received from customers.
2. Invoices received from suppliers.
3. Goods received.

However, it is possible to generate new forms of input as a result of your system design. For example, you might decide to send a form to each of your customers, asking what new products they would like you to supply. The returned forms would be another source of input to your system.

For many businesses, the main sources of output are:

1. The products of the business.
2. Invoices and statements for customers.
3. Cheques for suppliers.
4. Reports (information on how the business is performing).

Normally, it is the output from the system that will be most affected by the business needs that you have established. For example, the production of cheques might be carefully timed so as to use up full terms of credit. The reports produced by the system will reflect the priorities established in your business needs analysis, and will be particular to your business. For our example business, the interior design consultancy, a report listing the state of progress on each design contract might be needed.

So far we have looked at only a few types of input and output, in practice there are likely to be many inputs and outputs to even a small system. And not all of the inputs and outputs need be on paper. Goods purchased and sold will be inputs and outputs to your business. But most of the inputs and outputs will be *information*. Information may come on paper, by word of mouth, or be input at a computer terminal. Some of the information may be passed electronically to another system. For example, records of sales may be passed to a stock control system so that items sold can be deducted from stock levels. But at the time of designing the system you need not worry about how information is going to be transferred, it is important to know only what information is passed into the system, and what information is passed out of it.

The next stage in building your logical model of the business, is to make a complete list of the inputs and outputs. For example, the list for our example interior design business might look like this:

Inputs

Enquiries from prospective clients, definite orders for work, remittance advices, cheques, invoices, statements, sales tax returns, income tax returns, delivery notes, office furniture and equipment, stock items, consumable materials, bank statements, stock requests (from design consultants), details of new customers, details of new suppliers, details of names and addresses for mail shots, complaints from clients, thank you letters, account queries, letters chasing up bills, mail shots, trade journals and catalogues, returned customer assessment forms.

Outputs

Decorated interiors, design scheme drawings, design specifications, detailed design drawings, remittance advices, cheques, invoices, statements, purchase orders, sales tax returns, income tax returns, purchase ledger accounts, sales ledger accounts, nominal ledger accounts, fixed asset listings, requests for catalogues, enquiries to prospective suppliers, account queries, letters chasing up bills, mail shots, cash balance reports, cash forecast reports, sales breakdown reports, detailed profit and loss account with comparative figures and margins, debit balances by age and high value, stock levels showing slow moving items, Credit balances (showing separately those with debits on sales ledger), Price adjustments report (showing new price levels calculated from stock cost), detailed cost breakdowns, cash available for overnight deposit, bank reconciliation, stock reconciliation, bought ledger reconciliation, sales ledger reconciliation, invoices checked for payment, stock orders generated report, customer satisfaction report.

This list has been made up according to the requirements laid out in the list of business needs. For example, the input document 'returned customer assessment forms' may not exist already, but a document of this type will be needed if the functions 'Control sub-contract work standards' and 'Control material quality' (see Figure 3.1) are to be carried out. A corresponding 'customer satisfaction report' is included in the system outputs. Similarly, the document 'price adjustments report' has been included in the outputs because the function 'Adjust selling price when costs rise' is included in the needs analysis in Figure 3.1.

So, the inputs and outputs are a mixture of those items that must be there, such as invoices and cheques, and those items that we decide should be there in order to meet the business needs. You may be tempted to think that some system functions can be carried out without the need for inputs or outputs; for example the function 'control heat and light usage' might be implemented by using a simple thermostatic machine that required no input and produced no output (remember we are thinking about the system in general, a computer may not be involved). But for this function to be effective, a regular check should be made to ensure that the machine is working, and the check provides the output (it might simply be a tick on a list). If there is no output there is no control that a function occurs. It is essential that each function carried out by the system should produce some kind of record of the processing that has occurred.

Once a list of all the inputs and outputs has been made, the next step is to concentrate on each item in turn, and specify the minimum information requirement for each input and output (in some cases, such as for statutory documents, this will be pre-defined). You will not know at this stage what the input/output medium is (i.e. whether it is on paper, on screen or in some other form), but that doesn't matter.

When you specify what information inputs and outputs should contain, make sure that the information is sufficient for you to carry out the functions identified in your needs analysis. Where legal requirements are concerned (such as for tax returns) make sure that you construct a full and accurate specification of what is to be shown, and that all the information shown as system output can be constructed from the information passed into the system; if not you require another input (but think carefully, sometimes the information is already there even though it isn't obvious).

In the days when systems where designed from scratch, a complete, accurate description of all system inputs and outputs was essential. But with the advent of packaged software, it is doubtful whether this exercise is worthwhile. A report produced by a software package may be in a form that doesn't meet with your expectations, but if it fulfils your requirement, that is all that matters. For example, a description of the output document, 'Debit balances by age and high value' might be:

Specification for Debit balances report

Balances, aged over 6 months.
Option to order by balance or by customer.
Balances up to £1,000,000.
Up to 5,000 customers.
Credit balances identified.

It is not unusual for a system to be caught out by even the simplest of exceptions, for example a suppliers account showing a debit balance. There is no such thing as stating the obvious when specifying a system: a significant proportion of software faults occur because programmers take system users at their word - literally. It is time consuming, and impractical, to specify your requirements in great detail at this stage. But many pitfalls can be avoided by specifying precisely what format information should take; the length of text required, whether numbers can be negative as well as positive. And give the limits for how big a number can be (always allow a much bigger number than you think you will ever need - as soon as you constrain yourself to a set limit, a 'special' situation comes up that exceeds the capacity of the system).

When you reach the stage of having a complete specification of inputs and outputs, and you are sure that they are consistent with the business needs you have already identified, the next stage is to make a separate record of the sort of volumes that you need to deal with.

Types and Volumes

Whatever your business, every source of information that you have to deal with will fall into one of two categories: **Standing data** or **Transaction data**. Standing data is a record of information that stays more or less the same over long periods of time, such as the list of suppliers names and addresses, or customers names and addresses. Transaction data is a log of individual business transactions that occur each day, such as a list of the daily sales or purchases. For example, a record of stock part numbers, prices and descriptions would be standing data, but a list of the items of stock delivered on a daily basis would be transaction data.

Many business documents are made up of a combination of standing data and transaction data. For example, an invoice will have the customers name and address at the top of the invoice, followed by a list of the individual items sold. A system that produces invoices may refer to a standing data file to get details of the customer's name and address, and then refer to a transaction data file to get details of recent sales items. Holding information in this way is sensible; it would be a waste of space to hold a record of the customers name and address for every sales item - only one record is needed. On the daily sales record only a customer reference number is needed; when the system prints the invoices, it will look into the standing data file to get the name and address of the customer with the appropriate reference number.

When you write the specification for your system, you will need to know how much data you will process. The easiest way to do this is to make a list of all the sources of information you access, divide them up into standing data and transaction data, and estimate the volumes that you need to deal with for each type. Whatever the current volume of data, choose a much bigger number as the requirement for your system: if the system lasts for many years your requirements may increase considerably.

For example, the general manager of our example interior design company might produce the list shown in Table 3.1.

Some items, such as correspondence and petty cash purchases, may also use some system capacity, but if this is likely to be insignificant, they may be left out at this stage (we are allowing for large margins of error in our capacity requirements).

By the time you complete this list, you will be quite a way down the road of building your logical model. You will know what your business needs are, what your inputs and outputs will be, and what volumes you will be dealing with. However, we have concentrated very much on using an Input/output approach. We know *what* we want to achieve, but we do not have any clear idea about *how* we are going to do it. This is a sensible approach, as we said earlier it is the end result that matters. But to complete the picture, you must decide how things should be done.

Table 3.1

Standing data	Current amount	Capacity required
Number of customers	300	5,000
Number of suppliers	1,000	10,000
Number of stock items	1,500	15,000
Number of Nominal a/cs	50	200
Transaction data		
Number of sales per day	3	200
Number of purchases per day	50	2,500
Stock items per day	50	2,500
Number of schemes per day	5	50
Number of designs per day	3	50

Fitting the System Together

The best way to build a picture of the detailed business processes is to use the same method as that used by most DP professionals: flowcharts.

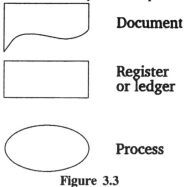

Document

Register or ledger

Process

Figure 3.3

A flowchart is a graphical depiction of the processes carried out in a system. Put simply, a flowchart shows what happens to the input in order to produce the output. It charts the flow of information through the system. There is no standard convention stating what symbols should be used for documents or processes, but it really doesn't matter as long as the person using the chart understands it. We shall adopt the commonly used symbols shown in Figure 3.3.

When you first sit down, constructing a detailed picture of your business can be difficult. So many different activities are related to each other it is easy to become confused. It is a good idea to start with a high-level picture.

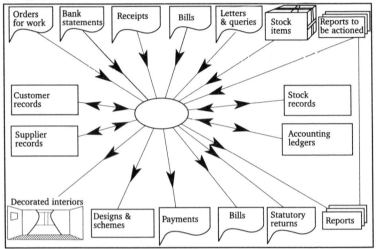

Figure 3.4

Look at Figure 3.4. This chart shows the main inputs to the system at the top, the outputs at the bottom, and the processing in the centre. The main sources of information (i.e. the information on customers, suppliers, stock, and design information) are accessed by the central process. Putting together a high-level flowchart should follow quite easily from the previous steps. You have already listed major inputs and outputs. The main stores of information you will have identified as standing data when carrying out volume estimates.

Once you have an overview flowchart, you can start thinking about building a more detailed picture. Your detailed flowcharts must show how the input to the system will be processed to produce the output. The goal is to produce a system that is as efficient as possible.

Many of the activities in your business cycles will revolve around the accounting system. Methods for handling accounting information efficiently have developed over the years to follow standard patterns. There is no need to reinvent the wheel. But you will find areas to improve efficiency where your business activities interface with the accounting system.

When you are designing your system, there are a few simple guidelines to follow:

1. Any information received should be entered into the system once, and only once.
2. Related information should be grouped sensibly for convenience.
3. Where possible, procedures that access the same information, should be carried out at the same time.
4. Information should be stored with the minium of duplication.
5. It should be possible to link up sets of information if they are connected by a logical relationship.

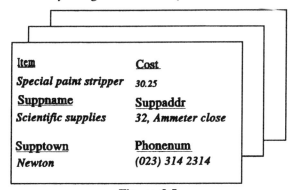

Figure 3.5

The first three points are no more than common sense. But the final two will benefit from more explanation. What do we mean by 'Information should be stored with the minimum of duplication'? Consider Figure 3.5, which represents a card index file of material available from suppliers. Each card shows a product description, cost, and details of the supplier. Now if the business used many items from the same supplier, the supplier's name, address, and telephone number would be repeated on every card for that supplier's products. If the business used lots of different materials, but purchased them from only a few suppliers, a huge amount of duplication would occur.

Now consider the filing system used in Figure 3.6. In this case, the materials information is on one set of cards and the supplier details on another. The supplier details are accessed by linking the information using a supplier code. Keeping the suppliers name and address in one place will also benefit other systems. For example, when purchase orders are produced, or when bought ledger statements are prepared, the supplier's name and address can also be accessed by these systems. The process of splitting up data to avoid duplication is often referred to in computer text books as normalization. Much of the pioneering work in this area was done by Dr. E. Codd at IBM, and further coverage may be found in books on relational databases.

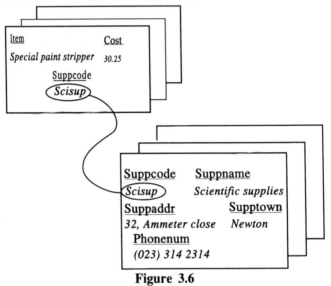

Figure 3.6

This explanation on data storage efficiency also goes some way in explaining why it is important to be able to link information. But linking information is important for reasons other than data efficiency. For example, if a design consultant in our example company was putting together a quote for a client, figures for material costs would be needed, and these could be obtained by linking to a materials register, or stock system.

When you think about a manual system, the concept of linking doesn't seem important. If supplier's names and addresses are held on a separate card index, then you can look at the index and read them. But when you are dealing with computer systems, things aren't so easy. Just because you have supplier's names stored in one system, it doesn't mean that they can be read into another system. And if they can't, somebody has to type them in - not what you expect from a 'time saving' computer system. That's why it is important to be clear in defining how your data should be structured at this stage; so that when the physical system is designed, these sort of problems can be avoided.

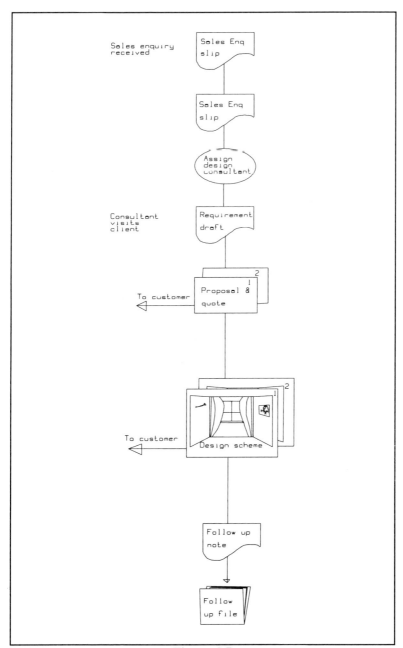

Figure 3.7

A good way to start developing a detailed system description is to split up the business into its main activities or cycles. You can often identify major cycles from looking at a high-level flowchart. For example, you can link up the inputs 'Orders for work' and 'Receipts' with the outputs 'Bills', 'Decorated interiors' and 'Design schemes' and 'detailed designs' to make up the sales cycle. But this isn't the only way. You may prefer to think of the output 'Decorated interiors' as linking up with the input 'Stock items' to form the production cycle. The important thing is to break down the business into manageable chunks in a way that *makes sense to you*. In most businesses Sales and Purchasing will be important cycles. Production will be an important cycle in manufacturing companies. Any related set of activities that form an important part of the business can be regarded as a cycle. You can build up a flowchart for each cycle in turn, and link together the charts for each cycle to form a complete picture.

Figure 3.7 is an initial attempt to represent the processing required for sales enquiries in our example company, the interior design consultancy. Sales enquiries are dealt with by sending a design consultant to the prospective client. The consultant prepares an initial proposal and quote, and creates a design scheme, illustrating what might be achieved. The decision is then left in the hands of the prospective client. If nothing is heard a follow-up 'phone call is made at monthly intervals until a decision is made.

The diagram does not show how all the various documents are dealt with, neither does it show links to other parts of the system. But it is a good start to developing a picture of how the sales cycle should operate. Note that the decision to produce design schematics for prospective clients is made for business reasons. The view is that the effort taken to produce the work will be paid back through increased sales.

The next step is to decide what should happen when a sales order is made. An expanded version of the flowchart is shown in Figure 3.8. When a firm order is received, details will be passed to the accounting system. It is important that this is done early, to minimize the possibility of revenue not being accounted for, and billed.

A copy of the sales order information will also be placed in the *customer information file*. This file will contains a complete history of dealings with the customer including the initial enquiry, and all subsequent work done. Organizing the information in this way makes sense, as the complete picture for an individual customer can be put together quickly. It also helps meet the objectives, 'Keep full client and product information', and 'Access information quickly', identified in the list of needs (Figure 3.1).

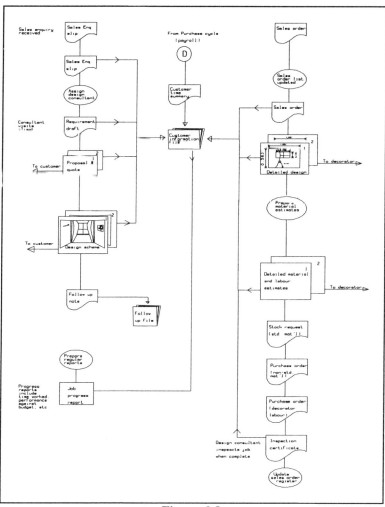

Figure 3.8

The designer produces a set of detailed drawings and instructions for the work to be carried out, including material and labour estimates. Stock requests are raised for materials held in stock. Purchase orders are raised for non-standard materials. A purchase order will also be raised commissioning a sub-contractor to carry out the work.

The list of needs (Figure 3.1) lists the functions 'control sub-contract work standards' and 'control material quality'. For this reason, regular inspection and reporting procedures must be built into the system. Inspection results are fed into the customer information file, and progress reports are produced regularly for management inspection.

So the detailed model of the system must take account of three things:

1. It must address the business's basic needs (which you will have already identified).
2. It must show how the system inputs are processed to produce the system outputs.
3. It must perform these processes in the most efficient manner.

Not all of the identified business needs can be catered for at this stage. Needs like 'produce high quality print' and 'lay out documents professionally', depend on the choosing the right sort of software and hardware when the physical system is designed.

As you start to sketch your ideas about how the system should work, you will find that you get new ideas about how the system should operate. For example you might start to draw a flowchart for opening and distributing the mail. As you do this it strikes you that it would be a good idea to log requests from customers so that you can check on how quickly you are responding to requests. This might not have been on your original list of needs, but if it is a good idea, what does it matter? Developing a system is by no means a perfect science. Often, as you work through the development process you will think of ideas that, ideally, you should have thought of earlier. You must be pragmatic, incorporating these where you can, and reluctantly letting them go when you recognize that to incorporate them would be impractical, or cause an unacceptable disruption to your schedule. This is where some of the 'methodologies' used by the big consultancies fall down; they treat system implementation as a theoretical exercise and sometimes fail to cope with the hazards thrown up by the real world. Your initial list of business needs must always be the driving force behind the development of the system; it is essential to keep your priorities in focus. But never expect things to go to plan, and always be on the lookout for new ideas.

Make sure that you have an accurate specification of any algorithms you may need to use. For example, project managers can use several different algorithms to work out the earned value of a project; or an accountant may be able to use several different methods to adjust accounts for the effects of inflation. In each case the project manager or the accountant will have to choose the most suitable method. You should review your system specification for any instances where an algorithm will be used and specify that algorithm precisely.

Before you finalize your requirements, agree them with your staff. Of course, there may be some areas of conflict between your requirements and theirs, but if you show a readiness to respond to their needs, they are more likely to accept yours. Many businesses suffer because staff see information available from new systems as 'a big stick to beat them with'. This perception can lead to negative attitudes and low productivity. On the other hand, if you ask staff what they would like out of a system, and actually manage to deliver it, not only will your business benefit from the system, but you may make productivity gains from the improved attitude of your staff.

When you have put together a flowchart for each cycle of the business, the final step is to draw these together into a final integrated diagram. (In practice it might not be possible to actually draw the diagram on a sheet of paper owing to size and space considerations. But you should be satisfied that all the constituent cycles fit together properly, and that no part of the business has been left out.) Figures 3.9(a) and 3.9(b) represent a final diagram for the interior design consultancy. Figure 3.9(a) shows the sales cycle and Figure 3.9(b) shows the purchase cycle.

For the sake of clarity, Figure 3.9 does not include all the inputs and outputs identified earlier in the chapter, especially in the area of reports, most of which would be produced by the accounting system. Procedures for dealing with correspondence and fixed assets have also been left out. However, the diagram does show all the main areas of activity, and the interaction between the various business cycles. When you produce a flowchart for your own business, make sure that *all* of the inputs and outputs you have identified are covered by the flowchart.

The flowchart itself does not answer all the questions, and you should make some notes separately. The following notes might apply to Figure 3.9:

1. Customer names and addresses are needed for the customer information file, the sales order register, and the sales ledger. This information should be held in one file, with a single update procedure (possibly done as part of the initial customer enquiry processing).
2. Supplier's names and addresses are needed both for the materials register, and the purchase ledger. This information should also be held in one file with a single update procedure.
3. Information common to the materials register and the stock ledger should be updated as part of a common process.

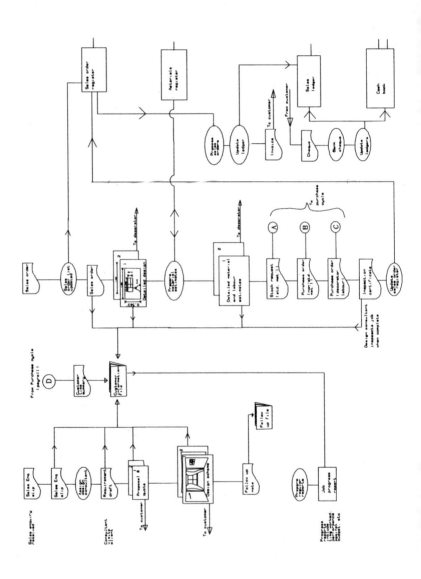

Figure 3.9(a)

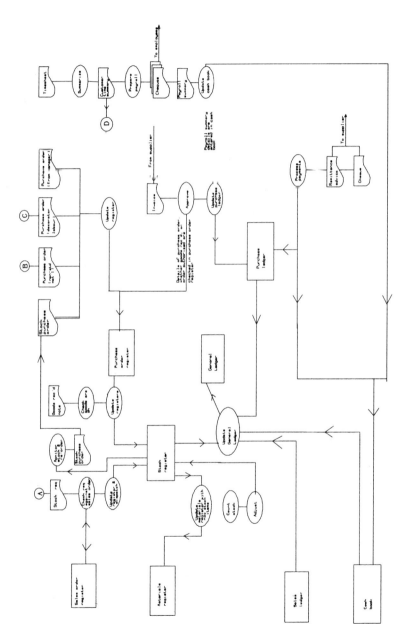

Figure 3.9(b)

Before you finalize your flowchart and notes, use the diagram to step through the system in your mind. At this stage it is difficult to see the system in detail, as you haven't decided what procedures will be dealt with manually, and what will be done by the computer. But if you can imagine all the procedures being carried out by the people who will be responsible in practice, an unthought of problem, or a bright new idea often comes to light.

At this stage your logical model of the business is complete. It consists of:

1. A list of business needs derived from the business's strategic objectives.
2. A list of all the input and output, with a brief description of the minium requirements for each item.
3. An estimate of the volumes of data processed by the business, broken down into standing data and transaction data, together with a generous estimate of future capacity requirements.
4. A set of flowcharts describing how the business processes are carried out, together with notes on the data structures and procedures.

Before we start reviewing the software that is available, there is one important step.

Choosing a Hardware Category

Once you have a clear idea of your needs, you can establish what hardware category will provide the most effective base on which to build your system. This book is intended for the small businessman, new to computers, and as such concentrates on systems solutions built around personal computers (for present purposes, the terms 'personal computer' and 'PC' may be taken as referring to all computers in the micro category, and not just IBM compatible PCs). However, if your business is of any appreciable size, or if you have to process large amounts of information it is not safe to *assume* that a solution based on PCs is right for you. Before committing yourself, carry out a quick feasibility exercise.

Personal Computers are limited in several ways:

1. The amount of data that can be stored is limited to the hard disk capacity of the machine. It is possible to buy machines with over 300 Mbytes capacity, and also use additional external drives. Until recently, the DOS v3.3 operating system could only address 32 Mbytes on a single logical drive, but new versions of DOS (such as DOS v4 and DR-DOS) don't suffer from this restriction.

2. In its native form, DOS is unable to use more than 640k of memory. The LIM 4.0 EMS (Lotus/Intel/Microsoft expanded memory system), which allows memory above 1 Mbyte to be used, is rapidly becoming an industry standard, but it is still dependent on software support, and is not completely free of restrictions. However, other operating systems, such as IBM's new operating system OS/2, and variants of the UNIX operating system (which include Xenix and AIX) are free from memory restrictions. As more software becomes available for these systems the useful power of PCs will increase significantly.

3. The processing power of PCs is less than what can be achieved on high class work stations, mini-computers, and mainframes. Performance improvements achieved in recent years have been staggering, but some applications may still require a bigger machine.

4. Personal computers, true to their name, are designed for personal use. However, local area networks (LANs) allow several PCs to be linked together. LANs have proved to be a very successful solution with many businesses, combining the convenience of the PC, with the resource sharing capabilities of the mainframe. However, LANs can only work well if the volume of data transferred over the network falls within certain limits. Where many users wish to have shared access to a common pool of data, a PC system is not a feasible solution (improvements in LAN technology are raising these limits steadily).

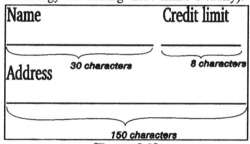

Figure 3.10

How can you get an idea of your capacity requirements? The easiest place to start is to work out the volume of data you need to store. We have already been through the process of identifying the likely volumes of standing data and transaction data. Your next step is to convert this into an estimate of disk space requirements. For example, consider the record in a customer file shown in Figure 3.10. The total length of each record in the file is 188 characters (30 for the name, plus 8 for the credit limit, plus 150 for the address). If there were ten thousand records in the file, the total amount of space taken up would be 10,000 X 150 = 1,500,000 characters. On a disk file, one character usually equates to about one byte of space, so this file would take up approximately 1.5 Mbytes. You can carry out this sort of exercise on all the major data stores that you have identified, and work out your total disk storage requirements. Bear in mind that often it is convenient to hold transaction data on disk for several months, so that queries can be resolved quickly and easily. If you have single files that are going to need much more than 20 Mbytes, you may have special hardware, or operating system requirements. If your total storage needs start running into hundreds of Megabytes then you may be better advised to consider looking up market from a PC (or consider a LAN solution, with your data spread of several machines).

If you are happy that one or more PCs can cope with your storage needs, the next step is to decide whether you will have exceptionally arduous processing requirements. The sort of applications that require this sort of power are:

1. Work requiring extensive manipulation of graphic images on large screens, such as heavy commercial design work. (This is often best carried out on high quality work stations; Sun are the leading manufacturers in this field.)
2. Very heavy number crunching, such as that used by scientists for analysis of data, or solution of equations by numerical analysis (weather forecasting being a prime example). Heavy number crunching applications are rare in most businesses. Computers used for these tasks range from mini-computers to supercomputers costing many millions of pounds.

If you are satisfied that you do not need this sort of power, then the final stage is to decide whether you need to share data between several users. The need to share data does not preclude using PCs, the use of Local Area Networks (LANs) is becoming increasingly popular, and often provides the best systems solution. But a PC network can only cope with a certain amount of concurrency before performance problems become significant. For example if you have a large accounts department where a group of accounts clerks all work together on the bought ledger system and a similar number work on the sales ledger then it is possible that problems would occur on a network system. The amount of general traffic flowing over the network would cause one problem. And procedures for protecting the integrity of the files (so that two users cannot update an account with different information at the same time) would also degrade performance. However if there is only one clerk full time on the bought ledger, and one clerk on the sales ledger, a LAN solution begins to look more attractive.

There are two ways in which data on a LAN can be organized. In the first, all the data is held on a central machine (called a file server). When one of the users on the network wants to access data it is transferred across the network and loaded into the memory of the user's machine. When processing is complete, the amended data is copied back to the file server's disk. The other method of organizing data is to spread data over several machines on the network. This can improve performance, especially if most of the time machines use data held on their own disks, but not all networks support this arrangement. Some systems cut down on network traffic by passing, not a complete file to a requesting machine, but only the information required. The way that data is organized on a network can have a significant effect on performance.

Let's take two examples of network usage. Imagine a system where several typists where using a word processor for letters and reports. It would not make sense to give each typist a separate hard disk. The information would be spread and difficult to collate, and the cost of keeping many hard disk machines would not be justified. The amount of information travelling over the network would not be great at any one time, because a data transfer is only necessary when a letter, or report is loaded for processing - a letter will fit comfortably in the computer's memory. And as each typist works on a different document, there is no danger of corrupting each other's data. However, if several bought ledger clerks were using a similar arrangement, the network traffic would increase considerably. The bought ledger will not fit comfortably into the computers memory, so frequent disk accesses will be required as each clerk enquires on different accounts. Also, as all the clerks are sharing the same information, procedures must be in place to protect data corruption, causing a degradation in performance.

If one bought ledger clerk and one sales ledger clerk were sharing a network, it would make sense to keep the bought ledger files on the bought ledger clerk's machine, and the sales ledger files on the sales ledger clerks machine. Using this arrangement, traffic over the network would be considerably reduced, as it would only be needed on the infrequent occasions when the bought ledger clerk required access to sales ledger data, and vice versa. (However, this arrangement may prove difficult in practice as many accounting systems will require that both files are stored on the same disk.)

If you decide that a local area network is a possible system solution, it would be well worth your while to read a specialized book on the subject, such as *Communications and Networks - a handbook for the first time user* by Phil Croucher (published by Sigma press), or *Using Networks and Communications Software in Business* by P.K. McBride (published by Heinemann).

One thing to be aware of: if you have a particularly inefficient manual system, it is quite feasible that three clerks working on a manual system could be replaced by one clerk working on a PC, making the expense of a network system unnecessary. But this sort of improvement should not be assumed unless a meticulous analysis shows it to be the case.

If you decide that your requirements go beyond what can be achieved from using PCs, you should take professional advice from a reputable consultant before making any decisions. (Small consultancies or individuals often provide the best service - you are unlikely to get a graduate trainee with little or no experience.) You may decide that even though your eventual requirements may go beyond what can be achieved using a PC, getting one will provide an entry into using computers. But, whereas it is true to say that most companies will find it useful to have a PC whatever their main computing requirements, getting one as part of an ill-defined, vague strategy is likely to lead to problems of false expectations and under-utilization. So beware!

The rest of this book assumes that you belong to the majority of small businesses that can build a useful system around personal computers. But whatever strategy you adopt, the considerations are similar, and people developing systems of all sizes should get some benefit from the book.

Summary of Chapter 3 - Assessing Your Needs

The first and most important step in developing a computer system is to produce a complete and precise description of the needs of the business.

Do not confuse procedures with needs - it is the underlying cause that is important, not the symptom.

Be creative in how you use the computer - break away from old constraints and use the potential of the computer.

In order to see where a business can use a computer, you must look at your business as a *system*, with inputs processing and output.

The stages in developing a computer system are:

1. Construct a logical model of the business,
2. Construct a physical model of the business,
3. Acquire the hardware and software,
4. Implement the system.

In this chapter, we saw how to construct a logical model of the business.

First, compile your list of needs by listing your primary business objectives, and break them down into subsidiary objectives. Create this list by thinking about functions rather than procedures.

Make sure that your business philosophy is reflected in your list of primary objectives. In this way it will permeate down through your subsidiary objectives into the day to day activities of the business.

Construction of the logical model should be driven by your list of needs.

Make a list of all the input to the system and output from the system.

Some of the inputs and outputs will be predefined, and some of the inputs and outputs will be necessary to carry out the functions that you have identified in your list of needs.

For each input and output, make a note of what information should be recorded, the size of the numbers or length of text involved, and whether numbers can be positive or negative.

Categorize the information that your business handles into Standing data (data which doesn't change such as suppliers names and addresses) and Transaction data (day to day transactions such as a list of daily sales). Make an estimate of the volumes of information processed for each type of data. Then estimate the capacity required for your system. The capacity required should be much greater than current estimates to allow for special situations and future growth (a capacity of ten times current volumes is not an unreasonable figure).

Specify how the business processes should be carried out. The easiest way to do this is by using Flowcharts.

Construct a high-level flowchart showing the major inputs and outputs and the data that must be accessed. Use the high level flowchart to help you identify the major business cycles.

Construct a detailed flowchart for each business cycle (sometimes you may start with a rough flowchart and refine it with successive attempts). When you have a detailed flowchart for each business cycle bring these together to form a complete specification of how the business processes should be carried out.

Make a list of notes to support your flowchart, stating the likely shape of the data structures, and highlighting where duplication should be avoided.

Perform a quick exercise to ascertain whether a PC is a feasible solution. You should consider:
     Data storage requirements,
     Processing power needed,
     Whether data needs to be shared among several users - consider
     a network.
If a PC solution isn't feasible; seek professional advice.

CHAPTER 4

Software

In Chapter 1 we looked at some of the basic types of software packages that are available, and saw how they could be of use to the businessman. In Chapter 2 we took a detailed look at what a computer is. And in Chapter 3 we developed a method for analysing the needs of a business. We looked at a business as a system, with input, processing and output, and we saw how to construct a *logical model*. Once you have a logical model, you will need to specify how it can be implemented in practical terms: you will build a physical model of the business system.

Some tasks will be carried out through instigating manual procedures, other tasks will be carried out by a computer. You must decide what computer equipment is required (hardware) and what programs are needed (software). Before you do any of this, you will need to learn more about hardware and software. We will begin this process in this chapter by looking at software.

There are two ways of acquiring software for your business:

1. Buy a ready made package.
2. Develop your own software.

We will start by looking at the sort of packages that are available, and highlight the important features that should be present. Reviews of leading software products are given in Appendix C.

In Chapter 1 we considered the three most common software packages for personal computers: word processors, spreadsheets and database systems. We saw how they could help with correspondence, accounts and filing. Utility packages like these are good for carrying out tasks which are separate from main stream processing. This is because they are 'stand alone' packages: not built to integrate with other business systems. For example, a common use of spreadsheets is to carry out analysis and modelling exercises in large companies. Data will be transferred from the main system (probably running on a mainframe or minicomputer) to a PC on a department manager's desk. The department manager can then manipulate the data without placing a load on the corporate machine. Common uses are producing analyses of customer balances, playing 'what if?' games: changing forecast figures to see the effects on cash flow and profitability.

Utility programs such as spreadsheets are well suited to applications like this as they are flexible, easy to use, and entirely under the control of the manager concerned.

The word processor is probably the most commonly used type of software, but word processors rarely integrate easily with other software. So, again, the primary use is for stand alone applications.

It is possible to produce invoices using a spreadsheet, so that amounts for VAT, sub-totals and totals are calculated automatically. And you could then use a word processor to produce a standard letter to send to all customers who haven't paid their invoices. But if you followed this course, you would still have the problem of posting the invoices to the accounting system, and producing a file of names and addresses that the word processor could access to produce the standard letters.

Wouldn't it be far better to have an accounting system that enabled you to produce invoices, post them to the ledger, and produce follow-up letters for unpaid accounts automatically?

When you are building a system there is a great temptation to acquire software one piece at a time, and then try and fit together the various bits and pieces. If you follow this course you will never have an efficient system. That is why in this book we look at software only after constructing a complete list of business needs and functions. We can then decide upon what software the business requires by considering the business's needs in its entirety.

Having sounded that warning, let's take a closer look at the three common packages.

The Word Processor

In Chapter 1 we looked at the general advantages that a word processor has over a typewriter in that a document can be stored, edited, and reproduced many times. But most word processors have a host of other useful features as well.

A word processor will have facilities for carrying out all the following functions:

1. Formatting text, so that the document looks properly laid out.
2. Manipulating text, making it easy to edit and restructure documents.
3. Help facilities, making it easy for the writer to call up on screen instructions on how to accomplish a given task.
4. Writing aids for checking spelling and looking up synonyms.
5. Mailing list facilities, for producing many copies of the same letter addressed to different recipients.
6. Printing facilities to make best use of a variety of different printers.

Let's take a detailed look at each of these areas.

Formatting Documents

The most basic feature that any word processor has is the ability to move a word onto the next line automatically when a line of text reaches the right margin of the page. In practice, this means that you can type continuously without looking at the screen (unlike a typewriter, where a bell alerts the typist to make a carriage return and feed the paper on by one line). This is especially appreciated by inexperienced computer users, as they can keep their eyes on the keyboard as they type. This feature is called **word wrap**. All word processors perform word wrap as standard.

When the writer wants to deliberately move down to a new line (for example, at the end of a paragraph), the **return** key is used (a name derived from the carriage return key used by typists). Most word processors use two types of 'carriage returns': those put in by the computer using word wrap (**soft returns**), and those entered by the writer (**hard returns**). This means that the writer can alter the document without destroying the format. If the writer enters a new word in a paragraph, the word processor will recalculate where the soft returns should occur, but allow the hard returns to remain, thus allowing the text to flow properly, but preserving the paragraph structure. Some word processors do not reformat text unless the writer moves the cursor back and presses the necessary keys. If you intend to make heavy use of a word processor, these word processors should be avoided.

Word processors also allow the user to align text so that the right margin is straight, which some people feel gives a tidier look to a document. This is done by increasing the spaces between words, and is called **right justification**.

One feature that definitely improves the look of a document is the use of proportionally spaced text. On most typewriters and printers all letters are the same width, so that small 'i' takes up the same space as capital 'M'. However some printers have the capability to produce letters which take up a space proportional to the shape of the letter (as used by newspapers and magazines). If you have a printer with this capability, and you intend to make use of it, make sure that any word processor you consider can handle proportional spacing (many cannot). And if you intend to produce proportionally spaced, right justified text (which looks impressive and professional) confirm specifically that the word processor you are considering can do it with your printer. If you intend to produce proportionally spaced text on a daisywheel printer, you should bear in mind that it can take a lot longer to print than evenly spaced text, because the computer has to send additional instructions to control the movement of the print head. (We will cover the different types of printer in Chapter 5).

The way a document looks is also affected by the placing of the text on the page. Most word processors allow you to control vertical margins (at the top and bottom of the page) and horizontal margins (at the left and right sides of the page).

A good word processor should also allow you to vary the margin settings, so that some sections of a document may have narrower margins than the main body of the text. This allows you to highlight sub-sections or lengthy quotes from other documents.

It is important for a writer to know where page breaks will occur, so that tables and figures are not placed overlapping two pages. Usually, the word processor calculates where the end of the page will occur and displays a dotted line (or similar) across the screen (it follows that there must be a way to enter the size of paper you are using). There is normally a facility to force a page break at a given point (used to start a new section or chapter on a fresh page). Forced and naturally occurring page breaks are often referred to as hard and soft page breaks (in a similar way to hard and soft returns). Some inexpensive word processors handle forced page breaks by inserting the appropriate number of blank lines into the text. This is a bad system, because any editing of text nearer the beginning of the document will cause all subsequent page breaks to move position.

Positioning text in columns (when showing tables of figures, for instance) is made considerably easier by setting fixed points across the page, called **tab stops** (or tabs). When the **tab key** is pressed, the cursor moves across to the next tab stop. There is normally a facility to position tab settings as required. On good word processors, text in tables can be made to align with a flush left or right side by using ordinary or right tabs. Columns of monetary and decimal figures can be aligned on a decimal point by using decimal tabs. Some word processors handle tabs by inserting the required number of spaces when the tab key is pressed, others insert a code recognized by the software as a tab (usually control-I, which is the standard ASCII code). The use of tab codes is much preferred to spaces, as, using this method, a whole table can instantly be realigned by adjusting the tab settings. A good word processor will allow different tab settings at different parts of a document.

Tabs are useful for aligning figures of tables, but not much help when you want to indent a complete paragraph. There are three forms of indentation commonly used in business reports.

The simplest form of indentation is a paragraph with a left margin that is indented from the main body of the text. However, this style is not very clear when several points must be expressed in turn.

1. A better way of making your points is to use numbered paragraphs, which usually take form of indented numbers followed by paragraphs which are further indented to the right.

Or, a style which is currently fashionable, is to start a paragraph with the first sentence at one level of indentation, and the remainder of the text at a second level of indentation. this style is referred to as a hanging indent.

The most basic word processors can handle simple indented paragraphs (sometimes by temporarily readjusting the margins). And most competent word processors can handle numbered paragraphs (usually by assigning a function key as an indent key which is then used in a similar fashion to a tab key). Although for some established products the handling of numbered paragraphs is remarkably clumsy. One of the marks of a good word processor is how easy it is to type a paragraph with a hanging indent (a worthwhile test of a product even if this style of presentation doesn't appeal to you).

Many documents are improved by the addition of a short label at the top or bottom of each page, and running page numbers. Most word processors support these features, and good word processors allow you to specify separate labels for odd and even numbered pages. Labels at the top and bottom of a page are called headers and footers. Headers, footers, and page numbers are not normally shown on title pages, and sometimes pages with diagrams, so a facility should exist to suppress them. A good word processor will allow you to change headers and footers as you progress through the document (for example, as the section title changes).

Leading word processors will allow you to produce text in columns (magazine style), and import graphics into the text. (Although, whereas graphics are seen as an advanced feature on the dominant IBM compatible PCs they are almost taken for granted on the less common Apple machines, which are designed to use graphics). There are many software packages available for drawing graphic images, and equipment is available for scanning and importing images from photographs or directly from video machines. If you intend to use graphics in your documents, make sure that the graphics software is compatible with your word processing software (good word processors support a variety of graphics formats, as do good graphics programs). The quality of the image you are able to reproduce will depend on what printer you are using. Good results can be achieved using a laser printer (although not up to professional typesetting standards). We will take a closer look at printers in Chapter 5.

Using the extensive array of features we have outlined above, anybody should be able to produce a professional looking document. But the real joy of using a word processor comes from being able to shape a piece as you write.

Manipulating text

Most written work, from a simple letter to a full length report is subject to some alteration before it is despatched. This normally means altering a draft copy and getting it retyped: a long process. And typing errors can easily creep in the second time round. With a word processor, only the alterations need to be retyped, and, because the original is safely stored by the computer, no additional errors can creep in.

But a word processor offers more than an expedient way of making alterations. To exploit the full power, you must change your method of working. A word processor allows you to move around whole blocks of text at a time. Because of this, you can build up the structure of a document sitting at the terminal. And you can then gradually put the flesh on the bones by adding detail to the structure. You can change the structure at any time by moving sections around. But this approach doesn't work if you follow the traditional course of writing letters by hand and getting them typed. You must take the plunge, and work at the terminal.

Many businessmen are wary of 'doing their own typing'. They think that it is somehow demeaning. They say they cannot type. But few people who work with computers have ever been taught to type properly (including this author). Once you get to know the keyboard, you quickly develop a proficiency more than adequate for your needs. And if you are going to take full advantage of the computer for controlling all your business systems, you will need to gain familiarity with the keyboard.

What are the text manipulation features that a good word processor should have?

One of the common needs of the writer, is to find a place in a document. Most word processors have a **find** command, enabling the writer to instantly move to the next occurrence of a given word or phrase. A useful extension of this facility is the **find & replace** feature that will not only find the next occurrence of a given word or phrase, but also replace it with another phrase entered by the writer.

Whole sections of text can be manipulated by using **blocks**. Most word processors, allow the writer to mark a block of text, and then move it, copy it, delete it or append it to another document.

Many people build a document by first sketching out a structure, then filling in rough details for section, and finally writing each section in detail. Good word processors have a feature which helps a writer to use this approach, the **outliner**. An outliner allows you to construct a document at several different levels. So, at the high level, you enter a list of major subject headings. Then, after the first subject heading you insert the detail for that section. Now, with a normal word processor, if you want to see the title for the section that you have just written, you must scroll back through the document. But with an outliner, you can jump up a level, so that the screen displays only high level headings. You can thus display the structure of a document without showing the detailed text. This facility is especially useful in the early stages of writing a report, as you can monitor the structure as you build it, and move whole blocks of text around simply by moving the headings at a high level. Unfortunately, some of the leading word processors do not have well developed outliners, so beware! If you are buying a word processor with an outliner, ask to see it demonstrated. Some otherwise reputable products boast to include outlining features, which turn out to be little more than automatic paragraph numbering.

Often, a writer working on one document will wish to refer to another document. Good word processors allow the use of **windows**, allowing two documents to be displayed simultaneously in different portions of the screen. Often, windows provide an easy way of moving or copying text between documents (by using the same keystrokes as you would normally use for moving text within a single document, but moving the cursor between windows as you do so). Windows can also be useful for looking at two different parts of the same document.

Advanced word processors have facilities for automatically working out mathematical formulae imbedded in the text, and sorting columns of text into alphabetical order.

With such an array of features available, it is sometimes easy for the writer to get confused. It is as well that good word processors usually have facilities to alleviate the confusion.

Help Facilities

As with all good software, word processors have a number of features to help the confused, absent-minded, obtuse, or misguided. Help messages are normally accessed by pressing a designated 'help key', usually one of the **function keys**. The function keys are a set of keys, whose function changes according to the software being used at the time (labelled F1 to F12 on a new style IBM keyboard).

Help facilities fall into two categories:

1. Standard help.
2. Tracking help.

Standard help messages will be the same, at whatever point the writer requests a help message. Tracking help will give a help message appropriate to what the writer is doing at the time. For example, if the writer has just marked a block of text with the intention of moving it, and then presses the 'help' key, the help message will tell the writer all the options that are available *for marked blocks*, and how to invoke them. Word processors with extensive tracking help facilities are much easier to use.

Help messages may be displayed in a number of different ways:

1. In a menu which is always shown on the screen.
2. In 'windows' automatically thrown up on the screen when keys for carrying out a command are pressed.
3. Only when help is specifically requested by the writer.

When you buy a word processor, don't be tempted by products that show extensive on screen help, with no means of turning it off. You will quickly become accustomed to the keystrokes needed to accomplish common tasks. When you write, it is easier to keep a sense of structure if you can see what you have written previously. Word processors that restrict your view of the document by cluttering up the screen with unnecessary text quickly become an annoyance.

Many products have different help levels. The amount of help displayed is then appropriate to the help level setting. For example, when help level one is selected a menu will always be shown on the screen, but when help level three is selected, no help is shown at all. This is by far the best system, as it gives a guiding hand to the novice, but allows the experienced writer to work unhindered. We shall take a closer look at the advantages and disadvantages of menu based systems later on.

Often, the most useful source of help for the inexperienced software user is a keyboard template: a small card that fits on or around the keyboard. These cards show the functions of the keys which they surround. Many of the leading software houses now include these cards with their products.

Writing Aids

Most good word processors include a spelling checker. These can be very useful for the forgetful writer, but they should be used with care. It is easy to write lamp instead of lamb, but the spelling checker will see nothing wrong in 'lamp chops'. So don't use a spelling checker as an excuse for not proof reading your documents. (Important documents should be printed before proof reading, for some reason it is harder to spot errors on screen.)

Features to look for in a spelling checker are:

1. The size of the dictionary (about 120,000 words is reasonable).
2. It should be possible to carry out a spell check while you are working on a document (on some older software, it was necessary to leave the word processor and use a separate utility).
3. The spell checker should suggest alternative spellings for unrecognized words, insert a chosen alternative, and automatically reformat the document (good word processors will automatically reformat anyway).
4. There should be an option to add unrecognized words to the main dictionary, or create a supplemental dictionary.
5. There should be an option to ignore an unrecognized word for every occurrence in the current spell check.

Some spell checkers include extra utilities not directly connected with writing, for example, the ability to solve anagrams, or fit words to templates with missing letters (useful for impatient crossword enthusiasts).

Good word processors offer another writing aid, the thesaurus. This allows the writer to call up a list of synonyms for a chosen word in the current document. Features to look for in a thesaurus are:

1. The way in which it has been constructed (this you can judge only by obtaining a trial copy, or reading the reviews in magazines).
2. The ability to 'chain' associations, so that synonyms of a synonym can be displayed, and so on.

3. The number of words used (although a well constructed thesaurus is more useful than one listing scores of dubious associations).

Bear in mind that you are only likely to make use of a thesaurus only if you frequently produce lengthy reports. Richness of features here are not an important consideration if you produce only the occasional business letter.

But what if you want to send the same letter to many recipients? Help is at hand.

Mailing List Facilities

Suppose you may want to send out a standard letter to all your regular customers, informing them of a new product you have on offer. It's an easy task to write a letter and photocopy it. But the recipient will not be flattered by the greeting 'Dear Sir or Madam' on a letter that is not properly addressed. And there are still all the address labels to prepare.

Most word processors have a facility that enables you to substitute names and addresses from a list, to produce many personalized copies of a standard letter (together with the address labels). If you are going to use this feature, it is a good idea to find out what format the file containing the address list should be in. Good word processors will accept mailing lists in several different formats. The key thing to check, is that the software that controls the data for your mailing list (probably a database or accounting package) can easily produce a file in the correct form for the word processor.

Printing Facilities

One area where powerful, and otherwise easy to use, word processors fall down is in the way they handle printers, often pretentiously referred to in the manual as output devices. Time after time computer users call software houses over printing problems only to be told 'nothing to do with us, speak to the printer manufacturer', and then after spending hours locating the phone number of the UK representatives (because the printer manual was produced in Japan and no UK address is given) to be met with, 'No, it's definitely a software problem, go back to them'.

Writers of manuals seem to fall into their most impenetrable lapses when writing about printers. And programmers seem to be equally struck when it comes to procedures for setting up printers. Perhaps it's because printer support is the last bit of the software that gets produced, and by then the programmers and technical authors are spending extended lunch breaks down the pub!

However, you can avoid these difficulties:

1. If you have a choice, don't buy your printer until you have bought all your software: you can then make sure that it is supported by your software, and meets your needs.
2. If you already have a printer, buy software that you know supports that printer.
3. Ask for a demonstration of the software that you are buying, running on the machine that you will be using, producing output on the model of printer that you have. Note how long it takes, and any difficulties in setting up.
4. Make sure that the demonstration covers all the things you will want to do, for example, using proportional spacing, producing full page graphics, using different fonts, use of a sheet feeder, printing over several pages.
5. Make sure that the demonstration printer is equivalent to yours. For example, if it is a laser printer make sure that it has the same memory installed as yours.
6. If you intend to produce draught documents on one printer and final documents on another printer (for example, draught documents on a fast, low-quality printer, and final documents on a slow, high-quality printer) make sure that the word processor can support more than one printer at the same time.

Now that we've covered the majority of features that a word processor has, Let's take an overall view.

General Considerations about Word Processors

In order to decide which word processor, if any, you should buy, you will review your list of needs (covered in the last chapter), and compare your needs with the capabilities of the word processors under review. (You will also consider how a potential choice will fit in with your system requirements as a whole.)

However, you cannot make a fair comparison between rival word processors by simply comparing what facilities each has to offer. There are three other considerations:

1. What size of document can the word processor handle?
2. How fast does the program work?
3. How much does the word processor cost?

Some word processors require that the whole of any document being worked on is loaded into the computer's memory. This restricts the size of document that can be worked on to the available free memory on your computer. Size restrictions can always be worked around by splitting documents up into several parts. But if you intend producing lots of bulky reports, or documents containing pictures (graphics use lots of space), it may be worthwhile considering a word processor which doesn't have this restriction. (If your computer has a large memory, this problem may not arise. Computer memory, and ways of extending it, will be covered in Chapter 5.)

Not all word processors work at the same speed. Whereas some will take you from page one to page fifty of a report almost instantaneously, others scroll the document up the screen infuriatingly slowly. Most computer magazines publish software reviews that include 'benchmark' tests, comparing the speed of one product with another doing the same task. If you need a fast word processor, look at the benchmark comparisons. But there is nearly always a trade-off: sometimes a fast word processor will not be rich in features, or speed might be achieved by holding the whole document in memory (as discussed above).

There are some word processors that work exceptionally fast, have a wide variety of facilities, and impose no size restrictions. But at a price. The most expensive word processors can be twenty times the price of a cheap word processor. If you are a professional writer, or you need to produce professionally laid out reports with formatted columns and graphic figures, then a top of the range word processor is worth the extra expense. If you produce a lot of documents, then a fast, well designed word processor, may prove more cost effective than a cheaper product. If budgets are tight, you may feel unable to consider one of the more expensive word processors. But beware of false economies. Do not buy one of the very cheap products.

A good way to acquire, moderately priced, quality software is to look out for 'out of date' versions of leading products. When a new version of a piece of software comes out, you can often buy the older version at a fraction of the original price.

Now that we've covered word processors, let's move on to new ground.

Spreadsheets

In Chapter 1 we saw how a spreadsheet could act as a sort of advanced calculator for calculations that follow a consistent format. Now we will look a little closer at a how a spreadsheet works. A typical spreadsheet is illustrated in Figure 4.1.

The concept of a spreadsheet was initially derived from the way that accountants carry out consolidations and reconciliations: they place all the figures on grids of squares, and then perform calculations by working down columns or across rows.

	A	B	C	D	E
1	Sales	breakdown	for	first	quarter
2					
3	Sales	Jan	Feb	Mar	Total
4					
5	Books				Sum(B5:D5)
6	Mags				Sum(B6:D6)
7	Papers				Sum(B7:D7)
8	Sweets				Sum(B8:D8)
9					
10		Sum(B5:B8)	Sum(C5:C8)	Sum(D5:D8)	Sum(E5:E8)
11					
12					

Figure 4.1

The spreadsheet in Figure 4.1 might be used to total the sales for the first quarter in a newsagent's shop. No sales information has been entered into the spreadsheet, it is shown as it would be created using the spreadsheet software. Notice that the spreadsheet takes the form of a grid. Each rectangle making up the grid is referred to as a **cell**.

Each cell on a spreadsheet has a label. The labels are usually derived by assigning a letter to each column, and a number to each row. In Figure 4.1, these letters and numbers are shown on the outside of the grid.

A spreadsheet program displays the grid on the screen, and allows you to enter information into the cells. There are a number of things that you can put into a spreadsheet cell:

1. Text
2. A number
3. A formula
4. A date (for spreadsheets that perform date calculations)

Text is used to annotate the spreadsheet and construct a framework. In the example in Figure 4.1, you can see that text has been entered to create headings, and indicate where the amounts for each type of sale should be placed.

So far, no numbers have been entered in the spreadsheet, but looking at the figure, you can see that the amount for book sales in January will be placed in cell B5 (so named because that cell corresponds to the 'B' at the top of the grid and the '5' at the side of the grid). Similarly, the amount for magazine sales in January will be placed in cell B6, and the amounts for papers and sweets will be placed in cells B7 and B8.

The spreadsheet will be used to calculate sales totals for the quarter by month and type of sale. If you were to do this job manually; to calculate the total sales figure for January, you would add together the amounts in cells B5, B6, B7, and B8. Using a spreadsheet, this calculation can be performed automatically, by using a **formula**. In the example, the entry in cell B10 is a formula requesting the software to add up the amounts in cells B5 to B8. Similar formulae in cells C10 and D10 calculate the sales figures for February and March. There are also formulae in cells E5 to E8, which work out the sales for the quarter broken down by product type. And there is a formula in cell E10, which calculates the total sales for the quarter.

In the example, where cells contain formulae, we have shown them. But normally this would not be the case. When you view a spreadsheet on the screen (or print it), it is the *results* of calculations that are displayed. So that when the proprietor of the shop enters the sales figures, the spreadsheet software will automatically perform the calculation, and display the results.

Spreadsheets can do a lot more than simple summation. Modern products have developed a host of features that make setting up spreadsheets easy, and enable sophisticated calculations to be performed.

For example, if you were setting up the spreadsheet in Figure 4.1, you would not have to enter all the formulae shown. First you would enter the formula in cell B10, and then, in one operation, copy it to the range of cells C10 to E10. But, you may think, the formulae in cells C10 to E10 are all different. Yes, but the software is clever enough to account for this (because it is the same calculation shifted over a number of columns). The next step is to enter the formula in cell E5 and, again in one operation, copy it to the range of cells E6 to E8. So instead of entering nine separate formulae, on this spreadsheet, you can do it in four steps!

A good spreadsheet program will enable you to perform more than just basic mathematical calculations; it will support many other functions; for example, trigonometric, logarithmic, statistical, text manipulation, logical, date and time, financial (for example: net present value, compound interest), and other special functions for manipulating spreadsheet cells.

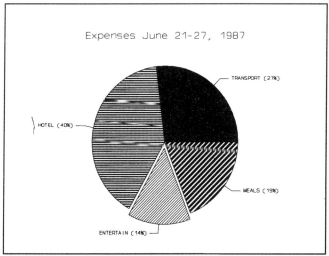

Figure 4.2

Quality spreadsheets will also give you freedom with layout, allowing you to change column widths to suit your data, and to differentiate between cells containing headings, and cells containing numbers.

One advantage that the pen on paper approach has over computer based spreadsheets, is that you can spread a sheet of paper over a desk to see a large area at once. On a computer you can see only as much of the spreadsheet that will fit on the screen (generally about twenty rows and eight columns). To compensate for this, good spreadsheets have a 'window' facility, allowing you to split the screen into two parts (windows), so that you can look at two separate parts of the same spreadsheet at once (or even work on two separate spreadsheets at once).

The commonest use of spreadsheets is to manipulate information for reporting and analysis purposes. (This sort of experimentation is often called 'What if' analysis or **modelling.**) Because of this most spreadsheets have facilities for importing information from files produced by other software products. And because information is processed for reporting purposes, heavy emphasis is placed on graphics. Good spreadsheets can produce graphs in many different formats (for example, bar charts, stacked bars, pie charts, xy graphs). Examples of graphs produced by spreadsheets are shown in Figures 4.2 and 4.3.

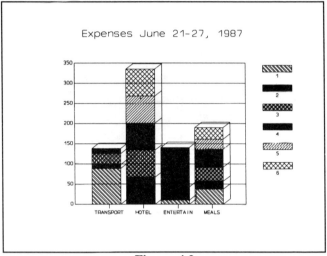

Figure 4.3

Advanced spreadsheets are able to apply complex selection criteria on the information held. Consider the spreadsheet in Figure 4.4. Suppose you wanted to know the sales for the London shop, or what was the average amount for a book sale, or which person made the most sales. With an advanced spreadsheet you could answer these questions.

However, if you need to perform these sort of operations with a spreadsheet, it is likely that you are using the wrong tool for the job. You probably need a database system (we will cover databases later in this chapter). So, what should you use a spreadsheet for?

Using spreadsheets

The most natural application for a spreadsheet is for modelling and reporting purposes. However, this type of strategic planning is more likely to be used in a large business, rather than a small concern considering computerization for the first time. In Chapter 1, we demonstrated how a spreadsheet could be used to produce an invoice. But in practice, this may not be a good use, as you would still need to transfer the data into your accounting system (which you could have used to produce the invoice in the first place). Another example we used in Chapter 1 was a cash flow prediction. A spreadsheet is

	A	B	C	D	E
1	Sales listing for newsagent shops				
2					
3	Date	Shop	Person	Type	Amount
4	1/1/89	London	Fred	Books	5.80
5	1/1/89	Boston	Dwain	Books	6.99
6	1/1/89	Paris	Marie	Sweets	0.75
7	2/1/89	Paris	Jean	Mags	3.50
8	2/1/89	Boston	Dak	Papers	0.35
9	2/1/89	London	Bill	Papers	0.80
10	2/1/89	Boston	Dwain	Mags	4.50
11	2/1/89	London	Bill	Books	9.75
12	2/1/89	Paris	Marie	Papers	1.60

Figure 4.4

excellent for this task, but if it is carried out annually, the cost of buying a spreadsheet would not be justified. So what is a spreadsheet good for?

A spreadsheet is good for carrying out a frequent calculation, that always follows a similar format, that cannot easily be built in as part of your regular processing.

For example, you would not consider using a spreadsheet for working out your sales tax (VAT in Europe) returns. This feature will be built in to your accounting system. Let's return to our example company, the interior design consultancy, to find an instance where a spreadsheet would be useful. For every design that a consultant proposes to a prospective client, he needs to give an estimate for the price. The calculation is as follows:

		£
___ sq. yds. of paint @ £0.5	=	___
___ sq. yds. curtain1 @ £4	=	___
___ sq. yds. curtain2 @ £8	=	___
___ sq. yds. nets @ £2	=	___
___ sq. yds. carpet1 @ £10	=	___
___ sq. yds. carpet2 @ £20	=	___
___ hrs. consultancy @ £25	=	___
___ hrs. fitting @ £20	=	___
Cost of special fittings	=	___
Sub-total		___
Add 10% contingency		___
Sub-total		___
VAT at 15%		___
Estimate Total		___

This would be a good application for using a spreadsheet. It is a frequently used calculation, following a consistent format, and the accounting system could not easily be altered to take care of the requirement (especially if it is an off the shelf package). The only numbers that the consultant would need to enter would be the amounts for square yards, hours, and the cost of special fittings. The spreadsheet package could be set up to calculate all the figures, save a record of the estimate on disk, and print off a copy to send to the prospective client. Time would be saved for the consultant, the typist, and the filing clerk; and less mistakes would occur.

If your information processing needs go beyond what can be accomplished on a grid full of squares (and whose doesn't?), you might need a database system.

Databases

A database is an information management system. This sounds like a grand statement, but a pocket diary, or a card index have equal claim to the title. But a database system goes further: a database program provides a facility for you to organize, enter, store, manipulate, and report on information.

In order to get to grips with how a database system works, let's think about how we use information. Most collections of information are organized around something. For example, information on salaries is organized around people. For every person that works for a company, somewhere, there will be a record of that person's salary, insurance number, commission rate, holiday entitlement, tax code, and all the other pieces of information that the salaries office needs to know. There will be a separate record for everybody that works for the company: one record per person. The salaries office will probably use a listing that looks something like this:

Name code	Job Title	Salary	NI Number	T a x
Fred Bloggs	Labourer	10,000	abc12345	20001
Mickey Duck	Director	95,000	xyz54321	1000d
Donald Mouse	Manager	20,000	ura99999	1500m

etc...

For information to be useful, it must be organized in some way. And if it is organized, you can put it in a list. The list of peoples salary information, we can regard as our **file** on salaries. For each person that works for the company, we have a **record** in the file. And for every record in the file, we have information covering a number of different **fields**.

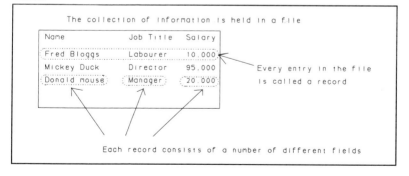

This is the traditional database structure: files, records, and fields. Most database packages work on the premise that data is organized in this way. You will recall from Chapter 2 that all information stored in computers is held in files. Database files are just one type of file. You could not display a database file and make sense of it, the information is coded in a way that makes sense to the database program (Database Files are sometimes referred to as datasets).

If you look at the salaries listing, you will see that the information falls into different categories. The name and job title are text, but the salary figure is a number. We will want to perform arithmetic on the salary figure (for example, adding up salaries to work out the wage bill for the company, or for each department). On the other hand we might want to carry out other types of operations on the text based fields (for example, producing a list in alphabetical order). Most database packages require you to designate in advance the sort of information that will be held in a field. Fields are given **Field types**.

Usually, the field types used are similar to the following:

1. Text (sometimes called character or alphanumeric)
2. Integer (whole numbers)
3. Decimal (decimal numbers)
4. Date
5. Logical (may only hold the values 'true' or 'false')

Another thing that you might notice about the salaries list is that each item of information (or, in database parlance each field value) has a limited size. You know that no salary figure will need more than 7 places before the decimal point, and that tax codes and insurance numbers do not vary in size. You may not be sure how long a name or job title can be, but you could be reasonably certain that thirty characters for each would cover most situations. Most database systems require you to enter the size of each field, so that space can be organized and reserved on disk.

To put information into a database system, these are the steps you take:

1. Define the fields, assigning each field a name, field type, and field length.
2. Define a file, assign a file name, and the names of the fields that will make up each record.
3. Enter the information into the system (How? We'll come to that soon).

The process is not always carried out in this order. Sometimes, you define the file name first, and then you are prompted for details of each field. In some systems, you are prompted for a key field. A key field is a main field used to identify a record. In the salaries file *name* would be a key field, as most of your queries on that file would be to do with the person's name. You can usually enter more than one key field. For example, you may need to refer to the file using the insurance number as a starting point. In this case you would make both the name, and the insurance number key fields. We will look at other uses of key fields later.

Some systems ask you to enter the maximum number of records that will be in a file. This enables the system to conserve disk space by reserving no more space than is necessary.

All systems must provide some way for you to enter information into the database. Screens used for entering information into the system are usually referred to as **data entry screens** Data entry screens normally fall into two categories:

1. On the first type of screen, many records are shown on a single screen, with each record occupying one line. As a record will normally contain more fields than can be displayed on one line of the screen, you are able to 'scroll' to the right to see additional fields. Further records can be displayed by 'scrolling' down. This type of screen is often referred to as a 'full-screen editor'. An example of this type of screen is shown in figure 4.6. (the example is taken from a dBASE IV screen).
2. The second type of screen resembles a normal paper form. Only one record is displayed on the screen, but all the fields for that record are displayed. Further records can be displayed to 'page through' the file. This type of screen is often referred to as a 'Screenform'. An example of this type of screen is shown in Figure 4.7 (the example is taken from a DATAEASE screen).

With both types of screen display facilities will be provided to:

1. Add records to the database
2. Modify existing records
3. Delete existing records

Some products give you a choice of either screen type. A full screen editor data entry screen is good for entering large volumes of data following a regular format, as it cuts down on the number of times you have to 'page' forward. This type of editor is also good for reviewing data, as you can compare several records at once. The screenform type of data entry screen is good for entering small amounts of data that cover many fields for each record. It is also good in circumstances where you wish to see many fields for each record at once. Most database products have a screenform style data entry screen, but many do not have a full screen editor. If your requirements are best met by a full screen editor, make sure the product you buy has one.

There are two distinct styles of database product. With some databases you converse with the system by selecting options on menus, and entering requirements on screenforms. With other database systems, you converse with the system by using a 'command language'. The modern trend is towards menu based systems. Ashton Tate's dBASE, the market leader and formerly the archetypal language based system, is now supplied with menus (although, you do not have to use them).

```
┌─────────────────────────────────────────────────────────────────┐
│ Records      Fields     Go To     Exit            5:26:49 p     │
├─────────────────────────────────────────────────────────────────┤
│ LASTNAME     FIRSTNAME  TITLE                SALARY             │
├─────────────────────────────────────────────────────────────────┤
│ Adams        Nathan     SALESPERSON          20000              │
│ Anderson     Debbie     CLERK                12000              │
│ Arlich       Kim        SALESPERSON          25000              │
│ Beman        Sandy      SECRETARY            12100              │
│ Bicksby      Hank       SALESPERSON          20000              │
│ Campbell     Linda      SALESPERSON          20000              │
│ Cohen        Larry      SALESPERSON          20000              │
│ Collins      Sara       SALESPERSON          20000              │
│ Daniels      Dominique  SALESPERSON          20000              │
│ DeBello      Todd       SALESPERSON          20000              │
│ Dean         Michelle   SECRETARY            14500              │
│ Dickerson    Lori       MANAGER              49000              │
│ Drasin       Pedro      SALESPERSON          20000              │
│ Drendon      Kelly      SALESPERSON          20000              │
│ Egan         Michelle   SALESPERSON          20000              │
│ Eivera       Harry      CLERK                10500              │
│ Garnett      Lena       CLERK                12250              │
├─────────────────────────────────────────────────────────────────┤
│ Browse :C:\. ..samples\ EMPLOYEE :Rec 1/47 :File : Num Ins      │
└─────────────────────────────────────────────────────────────────┘
```

Figure 4.6

```
┌─────────────────────────────────────────────────────────────────┐
│ EMPLOYEES                            Record found               │
│ Record 1 on screen                                              │
│ Name: Archie Bunker                  Spouse:                    │
│ Street: 704 Houser Street                                       │
│ City: Queens              State: NY  Zip code: 10069            │
│ Home telephone #: (718)-555-6754                                │
│ Social security #: 232-86-5755                                  │
│ Title: Salesperson                                              │
│ Payroll code: E3200                                             │
│ Salary:  25,000.00                                              │
│ Commission rate: 0.055                                          │
│ Sex: Male                                                       │
└─────────────────────────────────────────────────────────────────┘
```

Figure 4.7

An example of how these two systems work is shown in Table 4.1, which lists a comparison of the steps needed to carry out a simple query in both systems.

From Table 4.1 two things are apparent:

Table 4.1

Comparison of the steps required to list employees earning over £20,000 in a Menu based system (Dataease), against the same operation in a language based system (Dbase).

Case One - Menu based

Case two - Language based

Enter , 'dataease' to start program. Fill in security information on sign-on screen.

Enter 'dbase' to start program.

Enter 'use employee'.

Select option 2 from main menu.

Enter 'display fields lastname, firstname, title, salary for salary>20000'.

Select form employees from records menu.

Press F9 to select the reports menu.

Select option 3: 'Define record selection'

A blank screenform is displayed. You are prompted to enter selection criteria. Enter '>20000' in the salary field, and press F2.

Select 'define list fields' option from reports menu.

Another blank screen form is presented. Use the space bar to select which fields will appear on the report, and press F2.

Select option 1: 'Run report'.

1. Using a command language, you can do things much faster than using a menu based system.
2. Using a menu based system may take longer, but it is much easier for the inexperienced user.

Menu based systems are popular with inexperienced computer users. But do not be seduced too easily by a friendly face! If a person will be using the system frequently, within a few weeks that person will be used to a language based system, and will be able to make use of the flexibility that it offers. An experienced user will find a menu based system intensely frustrating.

On the other hand, if the system will not be used frequently, a language based system is a bad idea. When somebody wants to do something, they don't want to be constantly referring to the reference manual.

But don't be too keen to underestimate system usage, and talk yourself into buying a menu based system. Many businesses are a lot less productive than they should be, because salesmen have convinced businessmen to buy 'user friendly, menu based' systems. Multicoloured menus and windows look good, but they achieve nothing. In the long term, you are far better off buying a product with a drab exterior that performs well.

We've looked at the basics of setting up a database system, and explored the differences between menu based systems, and language based systems. But we haven't yet seen the full potential of what you can do with a database.

In our initial examples, we saw how you could store information on salaries by creating *fields* to hold individual items of information. You could then bring together this information, by defining a *file*, and including the required fields in the file definition. The file will be made up of a number of *records*, each record being made up of the fields you have included in the file definition.

In most companies there are many sets of information that need to be held. For example:

>   Amounts owing to suppliers
>   Suppliers names and addresses
>   Stock on order
>   Stocks details

Do you notice something about these sets of information? They are all related to each other. For example, when a cheque is sent to a supplier, the accounts department must know the amount owing and the name and address. When the buying department considers what stock to order, they must look at details of stock held (to decide which stock items are low, and who supplies them), then look at stock on order (to make sure it hasn't already been ordered), and then look up the suppliers name and address to place the order. An example of how this system may be set up as a database with four files is shown in Figure 4.8. The file names are shown in capitals, and the field names are shown as column headings. For example, the file holding accounts details is called BLED (because it is produced by the bought ledger system), and it contains fields called 'Acct', 'Balance', and 'Credit'.

Suppose that you want to produce a report on stock that should be ordered. Look at Figure 4.8, the file STOCKDET, contains the following relevant fields:

Field name	Description
Stk_code	This field holds a code which uniquely identifies each stock item.
Descrip	This field holds a description of the stock item.
Amount	This field holds number of items in stock.
Ord_lev	This field holds the level at which new stock should be ordered.

So, from the information you have stored in the STOCKDET file, you could produce a report with the following headings:

Stock code   Description   Amount in stock   Re-order level

From our example on menu based vs command based systems, you know that a database is able to select information conditionally, so you might make the report more useful by including only those items where the stock level was less than or equal to the re-order level.

So far, we have a good start in developing a stock order report, but can we go further? As it is, the buying department knows what stock to order, but they will still have to look up the supplier's name and address. It would speed things up if we could include this on the stock order report.

In the stock details file, there are two fields containing information on suppliers Supp1 and Supp2. The field Supp1 holds the account number of the primary supplier, and Supp2 holds the account number of an alternative supplier (if one exists). And in the Name and Address file, NAMAD, there is a list of names and addresses for each supplier's

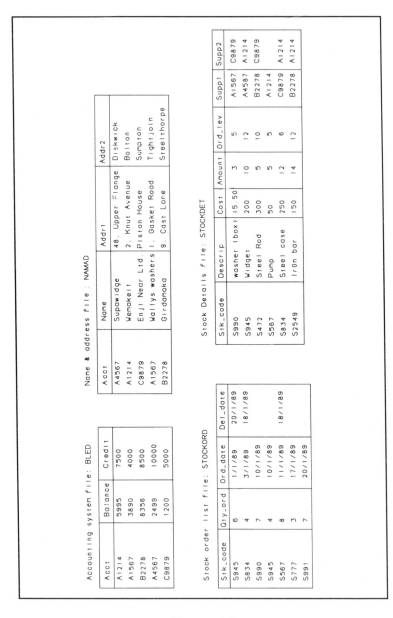

Figure 4.8

account code. If we could somehow link up the two files, we could produce a report that included the supplier's name and address.

This concept of linking is at the heart of a good database system. A Database system that allows you to use information from a number of different files by defining links between them is called a **relational database**. Originally this expression was reserved for database systems that met a precise specification (based on relational algebra from mathematical set theory) proposed by Dr. E. Codd. But eager software marketing departments have persistently misapplied the term for so long that now it is an acceptable label for any database that allows linking between files.

How does the linking take place? With varying degrees of difficulty, depending on what database product you are using! On a menu based system establishing a link is often straightforward. For example, using Dataease you are given a screen where you enter first the file names and then the names of the fields that you wish to link on. Some language based products make heavy work of linking files. In Dbase you have to go through a complicated procedure, accessing different 'working spaces' and forming links between them. However, newer versions of Dbase support a language standard close to Codd's model: SQL (Structured Query Language, pronounced sequel). SQL looks like the database language of the future, it is gaining popularity not only with PC users but also on mainframe and mini sites as well.

Let's take an example of how you could use SQL. Still keeping with the stock order example, suppose you wished to print out the Stock code, stock description, stock cost, and the name of the primary supplier. The code, description and cost are held in the STOCKDET file, but the name is held in the NAMAD file. Using SQL, the query would be written:

SELECT stk_code, descrip, cost, name
FROM Stockdet, Namad
WHERE supp1=acct

The words SELECT, FROM, and WHERE are standard SQL commands. SELECT specifies which fields you want to look at, FROM specifies which files they are contained in (although, in SQL, files are more properly referred to as tables), and WHERE gives the condition for linking. (The supp1 field contains the account code in the Stockdet table. We can match this with the account code in the Namad table, by looking in the Acct field.) The WHERE command can also be used to impose other conditions. For example, to restrict the report to those stock items that need to be ordered, the WHERE part of the command

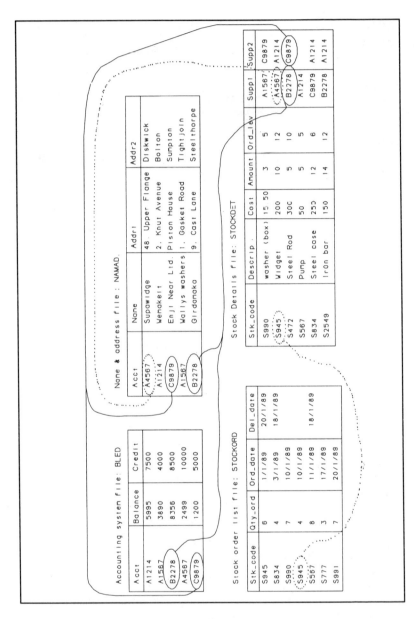

Figure 4.9

would be: WHERE suppl=acct and amount<=ord_lev (The operator '<=' means 'less than or equal to').

A relational database system gives you immense flexibility in the way that you can interrogate and report on information. Let's take another look at our stock order example, to see if we can exploit these properties. How do we know if we can afford to order new stock? Details of our credit limit with each supplier are in the BLED file in the accounting system. How can we make use of the information? By taking the following steps:

1. Find out how much new stock should be ordered. Let's say that it is company policy to order up to twice the minium level. Therefore the amount of stock to be ordered will be given by: (ord_lev + (ord_lev - amount).

2. Find out the cost of the order. This can be worked out easily from (cost x quantity ordered). Remember, we know the quantity ordered from step 1, and the cost is in the cost field.

3. Next find out what our credit limit is. We form a link to the BLED file, matching the supplier's account number in the Suppl field in the STOCKDET file to a value in the field Acct in the BLED file. We can then calculate the available credit by using (Credit - Balance).

4. Now, we compare the cost of the order (worked out in step 2) with the available credit (worked out in step 3).

5. If we do not have enough credit to place the order, all is not lost. We can perform another link, but this time using the account number for the alternative supplier, which is held in the field Supp2.

There's just one thing wrong with the system we're developing. What's to stop you ordering the same stock over and over again? Before raising an order for new stock, we should check that an order hasn't already been raised. We could do this by linking to the Stock order file, STOCKORD. But this time we will need to link on the stock code field: stk_code. If an order has been placed, and no delivery date is listed, stock is about to come in, and we don't need to raise another order. Examples of these links are shown in Figure 4.9.

The processes for producing our stock order report could be automated fairly easily using a language based system (such as dBASE). Most language based systems give you not only commands for interrogating files, but also a host of other functions for carrying out calculations, manipulating data, and controlling the flow of commands (for example, so that certain calculations can be repeated if conditions are not met, or to make the processing of some commands conditional upon the outcome of other commands). Sequences of commands can be saved as files, and run as needed. Indeed, the facilities available are the same as you would expect from any *programming language*. But because database languages are set up to be easy to use, with powerful commands, they are normally referred to as **Fourth generation Languages**. Many companies build their own applications using database systems. Indeed, you could implement all the systems you need for a business, by developing fourth generation applications using a language based database (and many companies do). But this process may require considerable resources, and, if your needs are fairly standard, it is probably a lot easier and cheaper to settle on a combination of software packages.

That covers the three most common 'stand alone' type of packages. As you might have guessed, buying a quality product of each type can be an expensive business. And for that reason, some software manufacturers have sought to entice customers with a 'package deal' whereby a number of programs are sold as an integrated package. We will look at some of these packages later. But first, let's look at some of the other types of software package available.

Desktop Publishing

Many people these days are using computers to produce newsletters or magazines, without any help or involvement from professional printers or typesetters. Modern software packages allow you to combine text in different styles and sizes with pictures on a computer screen, and print the result with reasonable quality on a laser printer. Desktop publishing has a done a lot to improve the face of some previously typed and photocopied journals. But there are some dangers.

If you are producing a document that will eventually have to be typeset professionally, it is often easier for the printer if you deliver a normal word processed file on disk, rather than a desktop published document. So it isn't *necessarily* a way of cutting down on printing costs. However, if you are confident about your page layout capabilities, and your system supports postscript output, you can feed a typesetting machine direct, saving much of the typesetting cost.

Don't expect to be able to produce the same quality of output from your desktop publishing system, that you previously obtained from a printer. Most types of laser printer operate at a resolution of 300 dots per inch. This may sound like a lot, but professional printing systems typically work in the range 1300 to 2600 dots per inch. And there is a big difference. Not only that, but there is an art in making up a page so that it looks right, and it is difficult for an amateur to produce a document with a professional look.

However, where the cost of professional printing is not justified, desktop publishing can do a lot to improve a document, and it is fun.

With recent advances in word processing software, you can achieve results similar to those produced by a desktop publishing package, using a product like Wordperfect. However, if you feel that you need a product with more depth, Rank Xerox's **Ventura**, has been at the top of the PC market for a long time. If your computing requirements revolve more around desktop publishing than any other area, you should consider the Apple Macintosh in preference to an IBM compatible machine. The Macintosh is designed to handle text and graphics, and in combination with the Apple LaserWriter printer produces superb results. (Many contend that Apple machines are superior to IBM compatibles in all respects, and it is difficult to disagree. However, the market is with IBM, and the range of software is much greater, as is the number of consultants who understand IBM computers.)

The DeskTop Organizer

A desktop organizer is a sort of electronic filofax with extras. Normally an organizer contains:

1. A diary facility: a monthly calendar is displayed on the screen (you may choose which month). If you select a given day, a 'diary page' is displayed, and you may enter or review appointments.
2. A calculator, similar in operation to a conventional calculator.
3. A 'scratch pad', for making notes.
4. A phone book facility, for recording and retrieving phone numbers.

Organizers generally come as 'memory resident' programs. This means that they can be loaded up into the computer's memory, and then 'disappear' until called upon with a special key combination. When called upon, the memory resident program will temporarily interrupt the currently executing program.

For example, you may be working on a spreadsheet application when the phone rings. You are asked if you can make a meeting next week. You call up the organizer program, and, as you speak, display your diary, fix a date, and record it on the screen. You are asked to bring a list of things, so you immediately switch to the scratchpad facility, and note details. Putting the phone down, you press another key, and returned to the spreadsheet program at the point where you left off.

It sounds great in theory, but some people are asked to make appointments when they are not sitting at their desk, and a diary fits into the pocket a little easier than a computer! But the scratchpad facility can be very useful. Some organizers allow you to export and import data from other applications (the examples of database editor screens shown earlier were originally captured in this way). The phone book facility is popular amongst some users. If you have the right equipment, some organizers, not only look up the phone number but dial it for you as well.

Borland's **Sidekick** was the original organizer, and is still probably the best on the market.

Computer Aided Design, Drawing and Paint Packages

People wish to produce pictures for a number of different reasons. Architects and engineers, want accurate drawings with proper scaling and dimension information. Producers of reports, and advertising literature may want a figure to illustrate a point, and enliven the text. Designers of computer systems may want an easy way of drawing flowcharts. Interior designers may want to plan out the new look for a room. Salesmen may want to develop impressive presentation slides, and analysts may want to produce various types of graphs. Any of these tasks can be made easier by using a computer.

There are four different styles of packages:

1. The CADD/Drawing type of package. This type of package enables you to create a design on the screen, and save it for subsequent output to a printer, plotter, or transfer to another system. A CADD or drawing package normally treats a drawing as being made up of a number of 'objects'. Each object is assigned co-ordinates and properties. It may be scaled up, scaled down, or rotated.

2. The Paint type of package. Again, this type of package enables you to create a picture and save it. However, with this type of package the picture is normally constructed from a large number of dots, the size of each dot being dependent on the screen resolution (these dots are called pixels). A new item is added to a picture by adjusting the attributes of the relevant pixels. Once the object is added, it becomes impartible from the drawing as a whole (c.f. the drawing type of package where each object retains its individuality).

3. The 'presentation' style of package. Images suitable for business presentations are created or captured from screens produced by other software products, and put together to make up a rolling

slide show. Some of these packages have output capabilities so that slides can be produced. Others are intended to be used solely for PC based demonstrations.

4. Management Graphics packages. These allow you to enter, or import figures into the system, and give you the option of producing graphs in a variety of different styles. For example, pie charts, histograms, xy graphs.

If you are chiefly interested in sketching pictures, the paint type of package is a good choice. Modern packages have many devices to enable, even the most limited artist to produce a reasonable looking picture. However, images produced by paint packages cannot be scaled accurately, and produce poor quality output (especially when imported as pictures into word processors).

If you want control over your picture, a drawing package is more appropriate. For example, if you are producing flowcharts, or diagrams for a book.

The CADD type of package is an extension of the drawing package. A CADD package will include many advanced facilities, for example: automatic dimensioning and labelling, the ability to build up a drawing as several layers, and facilities for defining 3 dimensional objects, and rotating them on screen.

The presentation and graphics type of packages are popular in big companies where the formal presentation is a revered art form. However, a small business may want to dabble with these types of product, perhaps as part of a novel way of promoting the business.

Communications Packages

A communication package allows your computer to communicate with another computer over the telephone line (you also need the appropriate hardware - see modems in Chapter 5). But why should you want to connect to another computer?

The most common use is probably to use an electronic mail service (e-mail), such as BT's **Telecom Gold** (in the UK) or **Dialcom** (in the USA). There are several services available on this type of network, primarily:

1. The electronic mail service itself. You can send messages to other subscribers of the service. Messages are delivered almost instantaneously, and the cost of sending them is small. A message can be sent to any number of additional recipients at no extra cost.

2. Telex messages can be sent and received through the electronic mail service. This is by far the cheapest method of getting into the telex system.
3. Fax messages can be transmitted via electronic mail.
4. Various information services are available, such as train and airline timetables, reports on public companies, an weather information.
5. It is possible to book train, airline and theatre tickets by credit card, and send flowers.
6. Free software can be downloaded (transferred to your computer).

Most small businesses who could benefit from e-mail services will do so more from the peripheral services than from the mail service itself. But as the number of subscribers rises, e-mail will gradually become a more viable alternative to the postal system (called snail-mail by e-mail devotees). One of the most cost effective ways to subscribe to e-mail is through **Microlink.**

Another popular use of communications is to connect to public bulletin board systems (PBS). These are messaging systems run by enthusiasts (called sysops). When you log on to a bulletin board, you can access a general messaging area, where words of humour, wisdom, and mindless boredom have been left by the world and his wife. The idea is that you comment on these messages. Then, when you access the system at a later date, you may find that your comments have been subject to the same devastating scrutiny as you inflicted on others. You may find some of the messages esoteric. But if you become genuinely interested in computers, a bulletin board is a good place to pick up the streetwise tips. Bulletin boards are also repositories of lots of free software. And some of it is good quality.

If you buy a communications package, make sure that it has error free file transfer capabilities. Data sent over the telephone is often corrupted. There are standard protocols that enable a computer sending a file to check that it has been accurately received by another. The two most popular protocols are Kermit and Xmodem.

Packages that you might consider are **Procomm**, or **Mirror**.

Project Management Packages

As the name suggests, these are used to plan and control projects. Most of the packages use critical path analysis to calculate when project activities should occur. Calculated dates are then used as a basis for assessing resource loadings. The better packages are able to re-schedule the project to make better use of resources.

The primary customers of project management packages, are major corporations involved in activities such as building oil wells and dams. But it is not inconceivable that a small business could fins a use for such a package. The top of the range product, Metier's **Artemis**, is prohibitively expensive for a small business, but you do get a lot. Its features include full graphics capabilities, and a combined relational database/fourth generation language that makes Dbase look silly.

If you see a need for this type of system, and you don't want to put a second mortgage on the house to afford it, you might want to look at **Super project expert** from Computer Associates, or **Harvard Project Manager** from Software Publishing Corporation.

Integrated Packages

An integrated package offers a number of software utilities in one bundle. A word processor, spreadsheet and database will always be included, some packages may include an Organizer, Graphics, or Communications facilities.

If you read the software reviews in Appendix C you may have notice that companies good at producing one type of product don't get a mention when another type of product is reviewed. Most good companies excel at a particular kind of software (though most produce a wide range). Perhaps this is why few integrated packages live up to expectations. However, for a company with limited needs, and little money, an integrated package can be the cheapest way of purchasing basic facilities.

There are a number of things you should consider when looking at an integrated package.

1. What facilities does the package have? Do they coincide with your needs?
2. Which parts of the package are going to be used most, and how good are they? (don't be tempted by an impressive demonstration of business graphics if you are going to use the package for the spreadsheet and word processing)
3. What is the level of integration? In some packages you can include a spreadsheet extract in a word processed document with a couple of key presses. Not only that, if you wish, you can keep it 'live', so that if you alter the original spreadsheet, the data in the word processing document also changes. In other packages, the individual components are connected only loosely.

There was a time when the relative merits of software products bore no relation to their relative prices. And although this is not so true today, it seems that a few irregularities persist in the 'integrated package' market. Perhaps because of a less sophisticated client base. So don't assume a package is good because it costs a lot. Conversely, some of the cheaper packages offer surprising value for money.

Surprisingly, one area where many packages fall down is in word processing. As this is the most mature area of the market place, one would have thought that experienced software houses would have all the specifications, and most of the code ready to produce a full featured word processor with their eyes shut. But software development is a chaotic process, and this is not the case. From the buyers point of view, this is a pity. Word processing is one of the major uses of computers in a small business, and a package with poor word processing abilities can often be written off altogether.

Accounting Systems

A general accounts package is probably the most useful piece of software a small business can buy. Utilities like spreadsheets are all very well for analysing numbers, and playing with predictions. But often these activities provide more of a distraction from the business than any genuine form of help.

An accounting system can help streamline your operations, by handing over necessary daily tasks to the computer. Gone are the desperate weekends when you finally get around to the paperwork. Dreaded activities like filling in a VAT (sales tax) return, become reduced to pressing a few keys. Well, perhaps Nirvana isn't achieved overnight, but it might be a step in the right direction.

What can an accounting system do? The good packages are capable of the following:

> Sales and Purchase ledger processing
> Nominal ledger processing
> Production of reports (monthly accounts & VAT returns)
> Stock control
> Payroll processing

A good system can be set up so that the minimum amount of effort is required to adjust the accounts. Most information should get into the accounting system by carrying out tasks that would have to be done anyway. For example, when an item is ordered from a supplier, the order form should be made out using the accounting system. Then, when an invoice is received, little work has to be done: most of the information is already in the system. When an item is sold, the customer's invoice should be made out using the accounting system.

The system will not only print out the invoice, but take care of all the bookkeeping entries recording the sale as well.

By using the accounting system from the start of a transaction, much duplication of effort can be avoided: a record of what has occurred will not need to be fed into the system at a later date. Retailers who deal predominantly with cash sales may wish to look at Electronic Point of Sale (EPOS) systems. In these systems, information recorded by the till, is automatically fed into the accounting system.

Good systems can also handle stock control. Not only will the system record stock levels, and adjust them as sales and purchases occur, but also produce reports warning of low stock levels so that goods can be ordered in time.

Apart from the time saved through using an accounting system, another one of the big advantages that a small business gains, is having access to regular reports. In normal circumstances, it would be unthinkable for most small businessmen to devote time every month to producing a set of management accounts, as big companies do. But if your information is up to date sitting in the computer, and all that has to be done is to press a button to get a report, you might as well take advantage of it. It is surprising what you can learn from stepping back and looking at an analysis of your performance in black and white once in a while. The reports produced by accounting packages are not confined to formal financial statements. Most good systems will provide an aged analysis of debtors, and print off chasing-up letters with mailing labels for overdue debtors (you set the parameters).

If you reach the stage where you consider buying an accounting system, it is wise to involve your accountant in the decision. But beware! Your accountant may have a deal with a software firm, and have an unhealthy predisposition towards one particular package. The important question to ask is: Can the system handle the processing from the inception? To answer this question you may need to ask others. Will it produce invoices, and automatically use the information to update ledgers? Can it handle order processing?

One practical consideration with an accounting package is to make sure that you can print invoices, credit notes, and any other necessary output on your business stationery. Some suppliers of accounting packages also provide the appropriate stationery packs.

Two packages with a good name are **Pegasus**, and **SAGE**. The Sage system comes at a number of different levels. The top of the Sage range, 'Financial Controller' is not that expensive, provides comprehensive facilities including order processing and invoice production, and is easy to use. If you are having trouble building a system that integrates with your present procedures, or have special requirements, you might consider the TAS+ accounting system. It is written in the TAS+ fourth generation language, and comes complete with the source code, so it can be amended to suit your requirements.

We've covered most of the common types of software packages in this chapter. But these days it is not only the individual packages that are receiving attention, but the 'environment' in which they are used. No, its not the temperature of the office, or even how nice your colleagues are that we are talking about. Its a question of man's interface with the machine.

Software Environment

In Chapter 2, we talked about operating systems, and mentioned the WIMP type of operating environment popularized by Apple's Macintosh, and emulated by such programs as Digital Research's **Gem** and Microsoft's **Windows** (WIMP stands for Windows Menus Icons and Pointers). Under these systems, a user requests actions (such as calling up programs or copying files) by using a *mouse* to point at pictures. (A mouse is a small hand held device that can be moved over the surface of the desk. A pointer on the screen follows the movement of the mouse. Actions are selected by clicking buttons on the mouse.) This is a completely different type of working environment to entering commands at the DOS's apathetic C> prompt (DOS is the usual operating system supplied with IBM compatible computers: see Chapter 2.)

Some claim that, as well as being friendly to new users, WIMP type environments improve productivity, as the user gets used to a consistent interface, and pointing and clicking is a lot quicker than typing. But there are some disadvantages to using these systems. They consume memory that would otherwise be available for programs, and some point and click sequences take longer than typing the equivalent command.

Much of the reason for the increasing popularity of WIMP environments is as much to do with human and cosmetic reasons as it is to do with efficiency. Put simply, they are more fun. (There are packages which do need to use such devices, such as drawing packages, but these are exceptions.) On the bottom line, running your programs through a WIMP type interface does nothing to make your computer a more efficient business tool. If you do feel more comfortable using a WIMP type environment, Windows is widely regarded as the better system (it is not expensive to buy). But beware! Not all software packages will run under these environments.

Operating Systems

For several years personal computers have run, almost exclusively, using the DOS operating system. DOS is unable to address more than 640k memory, until recently, could not support files greater than 32 Mbytes, cannot run more than one program at a time, and can not support more than one user at a time (although recent DOS based products circumvent these restrictions). Why is DOS still so popular? Because masses of good software is available to run on DOS.

IBM's new operating system, OS/2 (developed in conjunction with Microsoft, and biased towards a WIMP method of working) has a very small software basis. And an operating system without software is as useful as an engine without the motor car. OS/2 supports multi-tasking (several programs being run at once), but it does not support multi-user applications (several people working at once, using terminals connected to a single machine). IBM is spending millions in an effort to promote OS/2. But it is in danger of becoming a white elephant.

The product that will probably kill OS/2 has been lurking in the background for years: UNIX. Originally developed by academics, it is fast becoming popular in the business world. UNIX suffers from none of DOS's restrictions, and is not only multi-tasking, but a multi-user operating system as well. And there is much more UNIX software available than there is for OS/2. The only problem with UNIX, is that development has taken off in several different directions, and now there are various strands of UNIX. On the PC, three varieties are popular: UNIX system V.4 (from AT&T), XENIX (from Microsoft), and AIX (from IBM). Several efforts have been made to bring these systems together, but only recently has there been any real hope of a standard emerging.

Unless you really need the power of a UNIX based system, you are better off sticking with DOS for the time being. But watch out for Unix developments in the next few years.

General Considerations about Software Packages

In this chapter we have covered a wide variety of software packages. Some of them will be of use to your business, many may not.

Many businessmen, unfamiliar with computers, see what a package can do, and are so impressed that they buy it, only to do discover that they don't really need that type of software. The computer world is full of solutions looking for problems. And some of the solutions are very attractive. But many of these attractive solutions gave been concocted in ivory towers, and don't address practical business needs.

On the other hand (there always seems to be an 'other hand'), don't ignore software that, at first, doesn't appear to address the items on your list of needs and functions. The approach we outline in this book (List of needs → functions → logical model → etc.) is an approach that many companies would agree with. But few stick to this rigidly when they develop systems. You just can't expect to construct a perfect logical model, and then look for the software to fit. It is inevitable that you will see some software packages that tackle a problem in a different way, which in turn gives you the inspiration to alter your model (or even your list of needs). Developing a system is a messy, pragmatic process. We introduce method and order to reduce complexity. But never subjugate those powerful human qualities, intuition and feel. Yes, you must follow the guidelines, or you will lose direction. But keep a sense of practical perspective.

Many proponents of strict adherence to method will be aghast at this suggestion. The large management consultancies may not be happy to think that their rookie graduate trainees should use initiative, rather than slavishly follow the company checklist. But few successful projects owe their success entirely to the method used. If you feel that a less rigid approach is 'unscientific', consider what Robert Merton said about science:

> 'The books on methods present ideal patterns, but these tidy normative patterns...do not reproduce the typically untidy, opportunistic adaptations that scientists really make. The scientific paper presents an immaculate appearance which reproduces little or nothing of the intuitive leaps, false starts, mistakes, loose ends, and happy accidents that actually cluttered up the inquiry.'

Developing a business system is often very similar to the scientific approach (as Merton describes it!).

So, don't buy software unless you know precisely how you can use it, but don't dismiss a package lightly, you may be able to apply it creatively.

Another theme, that we have already visited in this chapter, is the modern preponderance for 'user friendly' systems. Many software firms put as much effort into developing a flashy user interface (with pop-down menus, windows, mouse control *et al*) as they put into the processing. Unfortunately, a flashy exterior does seem to sell products. Not that there is anything wrong with a flashy exterior. But you must ask, Where's the beef?

Another feature of menu based systems, is that they can be frustratingly slow to use, once you have acquired some mastery of the product (which happens far sooner than most people think). Don't buy a product which makes extensive used of menus, with no alternative quick method of entering commands.

But the most important thing about buying software is. *Don't acquire your software piecemeal. Decide on a complete range that will meet your business needs, and then buy.* Otherwise you have no chance of constructing an integrated, efficient business system. We will look much closer at how to do this in Chapter 6. But before you put a system together, you need to know something about hardware. And that is what we tackle in the next chapter

Summary of chapter four - Software

The major types of software packages available are:

Word Processors
Spreadsheets
Databases
    Menu based for 'Filing cabinet' applications
    Language based for efficient use and building applications
Desktop Publishing packages
Desktop Organizers
Graphics packages
    Computer aided design
    Drawing (object based)
    Paint packages (pixel based)
    Management graphics (Pie charts, barcharts etc. from data)
    Presentation packages (Slide show material)
Communications packages
Project management systems
Integrated packages
Accounting Systems
Environments (WIMP based)

Eventually, DOS will be replaced by OS/2 or UNIX. But unless you really need the power of UNIX, stick with DOS for the time being.

The important considerations in buying software are:

    Don't buy software unless you can use it.
    Don't dismiss a package you may be able to apply creatively.
    Beware of flashy interfaces.
    Don't buy menu based software with no quick alternative.
    Don't acquire your software piecemeal.
    Decide on a complete range for your business needs, then buy.

CHAPTER 5

Hardware

There are two essential components to any computer system. In the last chapter we looked at the 'intelligence' of the system: the software. But, just like a man, a computer must also have a body, the physical components of a system: the hardware.

A computer system will contain a variety of hardware items: the machine to carry out the processing, a screen and keyboard enabling you to communicate with the computer, printers for producing documents (letters, invoices, etc.), plotters for producing plans and charts, disk drives for storing information, devices for communicating with other computers through the telephone system, and many others. We will start by looking at the different types of computer available, and then go on to look at the sort of devices that can be connected to computers (peripherals).

In Chapter 2, we spent some time looking in detail at how a computer worked. Let's quickly review some of this material before going on.

A computer has two main functions; to store information, and to process information. Stored information is held on disks. There are two types of disks:

1. Floppy disks, portable and of limited capacity, are thin flat squares inserted into a slot on the front of the computer's system unit.
2. Hard disks, contain much more information than floppy disks, work much faster, and are usually contained within the system unit.

Information held on disk is organized into files. A file may contain many things (for example, a computer program, a letter, or database information).

All information is represented by either the absence or presence of a current, and because of this any information held in a computer can be represented as a series of '0's and '1's. A single unit of information (i.e. a single '0' or '1') is called a bit. A group of 8 bits is referred to as a byte. All counting has to be done in the binary system (which uses only '0' and '1'), and special codes have been developed to represent text characters, the most common of which is ASCII.

A computer carries out processing, by manipulating information in its registers, transferring information from its registers to and from memory, and transferring information from memory to and from disk. The processing power of a computer will therefore depend on two things:

1. How many instructions it can carry out in a second.
2. The number of bits it can operate on at once.

In Chapter 2, we explained the operation of the computer by taking the Z80 chip as an example. The Z80 was used on early computers using the CP/M operating system and operated at a relatively low speed, on eight bits of data at a time. (If you review the example in Chapter 2, you will see that every register held a binary code eight bits long, and that data was transferred from registers to memory eight bits at a time.)

Modern personal computers handle data much better than the old CP/M based machines. Information is handled sixteen bits at a time in most computers, and thirty two bits in the more advanced machines. If you hear a computer described as a sixteen bit or thirty two bit machine, it is the number of bits that the machine can operate on at once that is being referred to.

And modern computers carry out instructions faster. The speed at which computers work is normally measured by the number of times a computer chip goes through its regular cycle of actions (the number of clock pulses) every second. The Z80 chip worked at 2 million clock pulses a second, or 2Mhz (Megahertz). Modern personal computers work at speeds in the range 4Mhz to 33Mhz (faster if you categorize some of the more exotic machines, but these are in a different price category). Another measure of speed is 'MIPS' (millions of instructions per second). 'MIPS' differs from clock speed, as it takes several clock pulses to carry out an instruction. 'MIPS' is the traditional measure of speed used on mainframe systems, and it is only with the advent of super fast machines in recent years that MIP ratings have started to be quoted for PCs.

Now that we have our basic yardsticks (bits and Mhz), let's look at the sort of machines that are around.

IBM Compatible PCs

The IBM PC was a cumbersome beast, and virtually every compatible machine available today exceeds the original specifications. The updated model of the PC, the XT, was a sixteen bit machine running at 4Mhz, still deathly slow by comparison with most of today's machines. But IBM set the standard, and the software houses followed. There is more software available for the IBM PC/XT range than for any other machine. Because of this many manufacturers build machines functionally identical to IBM's (in fact IBM does not make the XT any more). IBM PC/XT compatibles (sometimes called clones) now dominate the market. But many manufacturers have produced machines much better than the original, at a lower cost. Most PC clones run at 8 or 10 Mhz, and are better designed.

The PC and compatibles use a chip that can address up to one megabyte (i.e. 1,000,000 bytes) of memory. As software became more demanding, the amount of memory available, and the slow speed of the PC/XT range became restrictive.

IBM introduced an upgraded version of the XT, the AT. An IBM standard AT ran at 8 Mhz, but cloned versions are available which run considerably faster. Another advantage of the AT, is that it uses the Intel 80286 chip (often abbreviated to 286), which can address more than 1 megabyte of memory.

IBM's latest offering is the Personal System/2 (PS/2) range of machines. The model 30 is an up to date version of the XT, models 50 and 60 are redesigned versions of the AT, and the model 80 is an upgraded version of the AT using Intel's 80386 chip (often abbreviated to 386). The great advantage of the model 80 is that the 386 chip is a thirty-two bit chip (hence the model 80 is a thirty-two bit machine - potentially twice as powerful as a sixteen bit machine running at the same clock speed). At the top of the range IBM are now offering a machine based on the 80486 chip, which is significantly more powerful that the 386.

There is one significant difference between the AT and the PS/2 range. In the PS/2 range IBM has introduced a new design standard called Micro Channel Architecture (MCA). The practical effect of this is that the machines cannot be expanded using the same accessories used for the AT systems. (Accessories are added by opening up the machine and plugging circuit boards into standard slots. These circuit boards are normally referred to as 'cards'.) This departure from standard has caused confusion among clone manufacturers. Some manufacturers have stuck to the AT standard, some have followed the MCA standard, and one group has even set up a rival standard. From the customer's point of view there is little to worry about, software remains compatible across all machines, and that is the most important thing.

Clone manufacturers have been quick to respond to IBM's lead, and it is possible to buy machines functionally identical to all of IBM's new models at a fraction of the price. (Although IBM now offers the model 30 at a competitive price through a high street chain store.)

The launch of the PS/2 range was closely linked to the development of the OS/2 operating system. The main advantage that OS/2 has over its predecessor, DOS, are that it allows a user to run several programs on one machine at the same time (**multi-tasking**), and it doesn't suffer from DOS's memory restrictions. However OS/2 does not allow more than one user to access the machine at one time, and the success of the system is still in doubt (this area was covered in more detail towards the end of the previous chapter).

Despite initial attempts to link the PS/2 with OS/2, it rapidly became apparent that the OS/2 system will run on the AT type of machine just as efficiently as it does on the PS/2. In fact the PS/2 range seems to have nothing extra to offer (apart from an expansion system, MCA, which is incompatible with the established standard). This is borne out by tests, where AT class machines produced by the more respected clone manufacturers frequently outperform IBM's PS/2 machines.

So, IBM compatible machines fall into three basic categories:

The XT class, including the PS/2 model 30.

Based on IBM's original PC. Modern versions considerably faster than the original, and selling quite cheaply now. Reliable technology with masses of software.

The AT (286) class, including the PS/2 models 50 and 60.

Faster than the PC, can use extended memory, and still able to run the majority of PC software. Very popular with business users. Good quality clones available at no great premium over XT class prices.

| The AT (386) class, including the PS/2 model 80. | 32 bit technology, the machine of the future, with a high price tag (cheap clones are becoming available, but should be treated with circumspection). Worth getting if you need to be at the leading edge. But as much current software is unable to exploit 32 bit architecture, not a required machine for the small business. 80486 machines now available, powerful, but *very* expensive. |

When you buy a PC, it is not only the processing power you need to consider, but what configuration (i.e. what options) you require. Most machines are available either with two floppy disk drives, or with one hard disk drive and one floppy disk drive.

There are several advantages to having a hard disk drive:

1. Accessing information on a hard disk is much faster than on a floppy disk. Consequently most programs run considerably faster on a hard disk machine.
2. The hard disk has a much greater storage capacity than a floppy disk. When you use a hard disk machine, you rarely need to worry about disks; all the programs and data are on the hard disk. But if you use a floppy system you will be continually swapping disks in drives.
3. A hard disk is less likely to get damaged than a floppy disk, cannot slip between desks, or get left in a briefcase.

In short, hard disks are highly recommended. If budget forces you to decide between an XT class machine with a hard disk, and an AT class machine with twin floppies, choose the XT with the hard disk.

Also, you must choose between a monochrome or colour screen, with either a text only display, or graphics. Working with a colour display is much nicer than using monochrome, but, unless you have a genuine need, it is difficult to cost justify. Perhaps the best course is to decide after you have seen demonstrations of the software packages you will be using, some software is much easier to use with a colour screen (and most becomes more tolerable).

Many computers are designed to support one or more of the four major graphics standards, but if not this can easily be rectified by fitting a graphics 'card' (a plug-in circuit board available as an accessory). Monochrome computers use the **Hercules** graphics standard. Colour graphics comes in three standards, which are, in order of increasing quality, CGA, EGA, and VGA. The VGA standard not only provides a higher resolution than CGA and EGA, but also is compatible with the other two standards, and so will accommodate a wide range of software (however the quality of the picture will depend on what standard the software is working to, only VGA software will produce a picture with VGA resolution).

CGA quality produces a recognizable picture, but the resolution is quite poor. EGA produces a reasonable quality picture, and VGA produces very good results (although even a VGA picture on an expensive monitor shows some irregularity with difficult shapes like circles). But graphics does not come cheap. The price difference between a monochrome machine with no graphics capability; and the equivalent machine with colour VGA graphics can be quite large.

Another important consideration when buying a machine is the number of available communications ports (used to connect to other devices). There are two types of port, **parallel**, and **serial**. Information is transferred through a parallel connection several bits at a time, whereas information travels through a serial connection one bit at a time. It is obviously more efficient to transmit several bits at a time, but this is not practical over long distances. So, in practice parallel ports are used to connect to devices close to the computer, almost always a printer or plotter. Serial ports are used for connecting to other computers, attaching a mouse, or for any other device that might be required (some printers use serial port connections).

Also important, is the number of **expansion slots** available. If you decide to expand the capabilities of your computer with an accessory card, you will fit it into an expansion slot. The more expansion slots that are available, the more freedom you have to upgrade. But this must be balanced against the capability of the computer. Some computers do not have many expansion slots, but have so many facilities built-in, that you may never need to use the expansion slots that are there.

There are other technical differences that separate one computer from another. You may see terms like 'interleaving', 'zero wait state', or 'RAM cache'. These refer to techniques used to improve a machine's performance. But if you want to judge the performance of a computer you are far better off reading the magazine reviews to see how it performs against others in bench mark tests. At the end of the day, what else matters?

We concentrate heavily on IBM compatible machines, but that's a reflection of the world as it is. Appendix D reviews IBM compatible machines that should be considered by the first time buyer. But an IBM compatible PC won't be the right solution for everybody, so let's take a look at the alternatives.

The Apple range

Apple's low range machines, the Mac plus and Mac SE have a distinctive look, the monitor, disk drive(s) and system unit being encased in one compact rectangular block, with the keyboard and obligatory mouse attached. By far the worst fault with the Plus and SE machines is the small monochrome screen, which seems almost ludicrous on a machine as powerful and expensive as the SE/30. It is not uncommon to hear users blame failing eyesight on the effects of peering at the small Mac screen. The expensive Mac II comes in a more familiar configuration, with a full size colour monitor.

When it comes to performance, Mac's have been leading the field for years. The 68000 series processors used in Macs use a 32 bit design, which is only now being used by the most expensive PC compatibles. Because of the sheer processing speed, and the way in which Mac's are designed, graphics handling is much faster on Macintosh machines, and the way in which the machines are used has been built around this. The Macintosh uses a WIMP (Windows Icons Menus and Pointers) type operating system, where the user selects tasks by using a mouse to point at pictures. And most Macintosh software follows the same conventions, so moving from one piece of software to another on a Mac is almost intuitive, requiring much less learning than making an equivalent transition on a PC. The in-built graphics support makes the Mac an ideal machine for producing documents including illustrations.

In a market dominated by IBM compatibles, Macs *have* to be better, and they are. But the vast software and support base for IBM compatibles will still be enough to persuade most buyers to stick with the PC.

Other Machines

Two machines that are becoming increasingly popular are the Commodore **Amiga** and the Atari **ST**. Both machines are based, like the Mac, on the 68000 processor, and have impressive capabilities, particularly in the area of sound and graphics. However, unlike the Mac the Amiga and ST are becoming popular as home machines.

Both machines are inexpensive, sold with no hard disk and one floppy drive, and targeted at the games market. Higher specification models are available, but these are overshadowed by the success of the games units. The Commodore Amiga, even in its cut down form, is capable of graphic and sound effects that will make the PC owner's jaw drop. Real time animation sequences, which would be out of the question on a PC are performed with ease. The Amiga has multi-tasking built into its (decidedly quirky) operating system (only now becoming available with OS/2 on PCs). However, as far as business use is concerned, these machines are facing an even greater uphill battle than the Mac. An increasing range of software is becoming available, but too late perhaps for the machines to shake off their arcade image. But if you have an adventurous streak, the Amiga 2000 might be the machine for you (and if all else fails, it will certainly keep you entertained).

Another powerful machine struggling for recognition is Acorn's **Archimedes**. This machine uses a RISC chip (Reduced Instruction Set). Because most computer programs spend most of the time using a small subset of a chip's instruction set, it was thought a good idea to produce a chip that performed these instructions only, but much faster. The theory holds true, and RISC chips have returned very impressive performance figures . (Some of the most powerful workstations at the top end of the market now use RISC chips.) The Archimedes is very fast, and has impressive graphics capabilities. Acorn's machines have been used extensively in schools in the UK, and they suffer from the 'educational' image. But the recent introduction of a Unix workstation based on the Archimedes might attract attention to a much undervalued machine.

Support

One area where computer manufacturers differ considerably, is in the amount of support they offer. The good manufacturers will offer 12 months full on-site support with a guarantee turn around time (i.e. the engineer will turn up within so many hours). An extension of support at the same level for longer than the 12 month period is usually available at a price (often quite reasonable). This sort of support can be invaluable. Another useful backup for the inexperienced user is the free hot line service offered by some manufacturers. If you have a problem, just call and they will try and sort it out over the telephone.

Once you have decided on a suitable computer (but don't until you have read Chapter 6!), the next thing you will be looking for is a printer.

Printers

There are several factors that distinguish one printer from another:

quality of print
speed of operation
graphics capability
colour printing
noise of operation
cost

No printer can perform well in all of these areas. For example, it is possible to buy a high quality printer, that produces colour graphics at high speed. But the cost of such a machine is many times what you would pay for a top of the range PC. There are several different types of printer, each of which has its own advantages. The main categories are **Daisywheel** printers and **Dot matrix** printers. Dot matrix printers can be further categorized into **Impact** printers, **Laser** printers, **Liquid crystal shutter** printers, **Ink Jet** printers, and **Thermal** printers.

Daisywheel printers use a mechanism similar to a typewriter: an impression of the character to be produced is hammered onto an ink covered sheet held over the paper. If a good quality ribbon is used, daisywheel printers can produce a print of a better quality than any other type of printer. Some daisywheels support two ribbon holders, so that text can be produced in two colours. But there are disadvantages to daisywheel printers.

Daisywheel printers are slow. Each time a character is produced, a wheel must be spun to place the character mould between the hammer and the ribbon. Because a specific mould must be available for each character, no graphics are possible. And support for colour printing is limited by the design of the machine; using more than two colours is cumbersome and depends on ribbons available.

On a dot matrix printer each character is composed of a number of dots. Because of this, characters of any shape are possible, and graphic images can be printed. The quality of the image depends on the number of dots that are used to make up each character. Speed of operation, and support for colour depend on which printing mechanism is used.

Impact printers use a print head consisting of a bunch of needles arranged in a grid. To produce an image, some of these needles are pushed out to form a character, or part of a graphic, and hammered against a ribbon, in a similar method to that used for daisywheel printers. This process is then repeated at successive positions across the page. Because all of the moving parts are within a small print head, much greater speeds can be achieved than with daisy wheel printers.

The quality of the print depends on the number of needles used to make up the print head. Low quality printers use a 9 by 9 grid, better quality printers use a 24 by 24 grid. But the quality of image is also affected by the production method. Because the print head is not a single moulding, the image produced is never as consistent as that produced by other printing methods (some impact printers have a higher resolution than laser printers, but the quality of image produced by a laser is much better). Coloured images can be produced on multi-ribboned printers, but the variety of hues obtainable is not as good as can be achieved with other printing methods.

Laser printers also build up images from dots, but otherwise work in a completely different way to impact printers. A laser beam is used to trace an image on a selenium drum. Exposure to light causes selenium to become electrically charged. And this charge is used to attract toner on to the paper and form an image. This method produces an even print density. Most laser printers work at a resolution of 300 dots per inch, enabling a high quality image to be produced. (However this there is still a noticeable difference between laser printer output, and professional typesetting equipment, which uses a density of 1200 to 2400 dots per inch). Laser printers are quick, and can produce good quality text and graphics, making them ideal for business reports, newsletters, or any documents that should look professional or require illustrations. Laser printers are, however, considerably more expensive than daisywheel or dot matrix printers, and (except for a few very expensive machines) do not produce output in colour.

Liquid crystal shutter printers are a fairly recent innovation. They work in a similar way to laser printers, except that instead of using a laser beam, light is shone through an array of liquid crystal shutters (liquid crystals are also used for the display on digital watches). Manufacturers of liquid crystal printers claim that the method is more reliable than laser printing, and that better resolution is available at the extremities of the paper (because the light beam is always at right angles to the paper, whereas a laser beam is at an angle). There is certainly no discernible difference in quality with liquid crystal printers, and the cost is lower than a laser printer. Liquid crystal printers are also more compact than lasers. The technology holds much promise. Liquid crystal printers could become the standard office printer of the future.

Ink jet printers form images by squirting jets of ink at the paper. As with all dot matrix printers, the jets of ink form individual dots, which together make up the image. The resolution of ink jet printers, is normally less than that of a laser printer (usually about 150 dots per inch), and they are slower in operation. Ink jet printers can produce colour output, and present an affordable option if colour is required and budgets are tight.

Thermal printers make up images by heating areas of the page, which then attract toner, making up the image in a similar way to a dot matrix or ink jet printer. Thermal printers are generally slow, and require special paper. The cheaper thermal printers operate at a lower density than laser printers. However, the better thermal printers can print at 300 dots per inch, or more, in full colour. If you wish to produce high quality colour images, a good thermal printer is one of the few options available (but these are expensive, probably a lot more than you paid for your PC!).

Plotters

Plotters work by using a pen to draw on the paper. An arm picks up the pen, and moves it across the paper, either through control of the arm, or by moving the paper on rollers. The arm can switch between pens to produce output in various colours (most plotters have a 6 or 8 pen carousel).

Plotters can produce high-quality, accurate output, and are used extensively by designers. Plotted output can also be very useful for management reports requiring graphics (such as pie charts or histograms) and are also used by project managers for producing critical path networks.

Depending on the amount of detail, a plotter can often produce a drawing quicker than a printer, as the pen has only to move where the drawing is, whereas a dot matrix printer will pass evenly over the whole page area. However, the resolution of a plotted drawing is limited by the thickness of the pen. And the number of colours available depends on the size of the carousel, whereas a good quality colour printer can generate an infinite amount of colours.

The cost of a plotter usually depends on the size, and type, of paper that it takes. Most plotters take cut sheets, but some take roll feed paper, which can be very useful for long thin plots (such as critical path networks). Professional design companies often need to plot on large sheets of paper, and these plotters can be very expensive. However, plotters taking A4 or A3 paper sizes can be obtained at reasonable prices. Most software that supports plotters uses the Hewlett Packard **HPGL** language to send plot details, and any plotter you buy should support this convention. Plotter manufacturers worth considering are Hewlett Packard, or **Roland,** who produce reasonable quality clones. If you need a high quality plotter Bruning's **Zeta** range take roll feed paper. These are established plotters (popular in mainframe environments), but can be quite expensive.

Modems

A Modem is used to connect to other computers via the telephone line. Most modern modems have one lead that plugs into the serial port of your PC, and another that plugs straight into a standard telephone socket. Some modems have an additional socket, enabling a telephone to share the same line. Older style modems, did not plug directly into the telephone system, but instead used acoustic couplers: rubber cups that fitted over the telephone's mouthpiece and earpiece. Some older modems also required you to dial a line manually (making a telephone a necessity), but most modern devices support automatic dialling.

Some employees of large companies use software that enables the PC at home to act as a terminal connected via a modem to the company's mainframe computer. But why should a small businessman need a modem? There are many services that are now open to computer users with a modem, mostly through electronic mail companies.

When you subscribe to an electronic mail (e-mail) service, you are given a password that allows you to access a central computer and facilities to send mail to other users of the system. The mail is sent to the recipient within seconds of you typing in the message, and is often cheaper than the conventional post. You also have the facility to send the same mail message simultaneously to any number of system users, at no extra charge. But such a system is only of use if the people you want to communicate with are also subscribers. Businesses using e-mail services may be in the minority now, but the number of subscribers is already large, and growing, so it is not a medium to be dismissed. And if the prospect of e-mail doesn't attract you, there are a number of other services available that might. For example, on the Microlink service, there are:

> Telex, Fax, and telemessage facilities (access through e-mail is by far the cheapest way to get on the telex system)
> Company search services.
> Airline and theatre booking services
> Bulletin board services to exchange views between subscribers
> Weather reports
> Interflora
> Special interest sections for PC users
> Free software that can be 'downloaded' over the telephone

Access to e-mail is cheap, and the range of services available to subscribers is expanding. Once you have a modem, you will also be able to access public bulletin board services. These services are run by computer enthusiasts, and act as a forum for discussion and exchange of public domain software (i.e. software with no copyright restrictions).

If you decide to buy a modem, you will also need to purchase appropriate communications software, and it can pay to consider the purchase as a package, as some dealers offer an all inclusive price, including registration to an e-mail service. **Microlink** provide what is probably the best service in the UK.

There are a number of technical terms associated with modems. The **baud** rate is the speed at which one modem communicates with another, common speeds are 300, 1200, 2400 and 9600 baud. Transmission may be **half-duplex** (synchronised two way transmission), or **full-duplex** (simultaneous two-way transmission). So a 1200/1200 communication link is operating at 1200 baud in both directions. If you wish to use the prestel service, you will need a modem that supports a 1200/75 link. You should buy a modem that supports at least 1200/1200 full duplex transmission. Modems to consider are, the Miracle Technologies **WS** series for most use, and the **Dowty Quattro**, for regular communications work. At the low cost end of the market **Amstrad** have a modem that supports speeds to 2400 at a very reasonable price.

Other Peripherals

We have covered the most common peripheral devices found connected to a PC, let's take a brief look at some of the others.

Memory extension systems are used to allow software with heavy processing requirements to access more than the 640k of memory available to DOS. The Lotus-Intel-Microsoft Expanded memory system (LIM EMS) has become a standard, and is increasingly being used by resource hungry software, such as CADD packages.

The tedious process of backing up information from hard disk onto floppies can be avoided using a **Tape streamer** system, that saves the entire contents of the disk on a tape cartridge.

Digitizer tablets are an alternative to a mouse for CADD applications. The user has a pen like device which is used on a tablet, making tracing operations possible. Digitizers allow more accuracy than mouse based input, and are more natural to use.

Your PC can emulate a Facsimile machine using a **Fax card**. However, performance and facilities are unlikely to seriously rival a dedicated fax machine. However it could be a cheap way into the fax club.

External disk drives, allow you to easily exchange data between 3½" and 5¼" disk formats. External hard disks can increase your storage capabilities.

In this chapter we have looked at the hardware available. In Chapter 6, we will find out how to choose the right Hardware and Software for your system.

Summary of Chapter Five - Hardware

Personal computers

IBM compatibles

> PC/XT compatibles - industry standard, underpowered, run DOS. 80286 based AT compatibles - industry standard, more power, run DOS and OS/2.
> 80386 based AT compatibles - industry standard, very powerful, run DOS. and OS/2, the machines of the future.

The Apple Mac

> Powerful, easy to use, expensive, without the large user base of IBM compatibles.

Commodore Amiga, & Atari ST

> Interesting machines, particularly the Amiga, but struggling to shake off the arcade image.

Printers

> Daisy wheel - high quality print, no graphics, slow, noisy.
> Dot matrix - faster than a daisywheel, flexible, cheap, inferior quality print, mixes text and graphics.
> Laser/Liquid crystal shutter - very fast, good quality, no colour, expensive, incorporates text and graphics on one page.
> Ink jet - relatively cheap, supports colour, mixture of text and graphics.
> Thermal - good for high quality colour, but avoid otherwise.

Plotters

> High quality, accurate, reasonably priced.
> Definition limited by pen size, colours restricted to available pens.

Modems

Allow access to electronic mail service, cheap way to get on telex network, availability of other services, public bulletin boards.

Other peripherals

Extended memory systems - increase the available memory for machine intensive applications.
Tape streamer - allow easy back up of hard disks.
Fax card - limited facilities, but a cheap way into the fax network.
Digitizer tablets - for accurate cadd work.
External disk drives - to increase storage.

CHAPTER 6

Designing the System

In Chapter Three, we found out how to build a *logical model* of a business. The logical model is represented by the following documents:

1. A list of business needs derived from the business's strategic objectives.
2. A list of all the input and output, with a brief description of the minium requirements for each item.
3. An estimate of the volumes of data processed by the business, broken down into standing data and transaction data, together with a generous estimate of future capacity requirements.
4. A set of flowcharts describing how the business processes are carried out, together with notes on the data structures and procedures.

To convert this logical model into a description of a physical system we need to know what software and hardware is available. We have already reviewed these areas in Chapters 4 and 5.

Now we are in a position to construct a physical system model. We can decide exactly how each of the business processes are to be carried out. Let's start by looking at the options available.

Strategy

The decision to computerize is never straightforward, and often there is no 'right' solution. But the more aware you are of the options that are available, the more likely you are to embark on a successful course. You must address several major questions:

Can I benefit from using a computer?
If so, can I use packaged software?
If no package is available, how do I build my own system?

You may think that the decision as to whether you should use a computer is already taken. But using a computer is not always the best solution to a business problem, and many business mistakes have arisen by ignoring this basic question.

There is a tendency for businesses to use new machinery or techniques just because they are fashionable. For example, many software vendors, and corporate computer users are now developing computer based training (CBT) courses. The question asked of training consultants is not, "What sort of training do we need?" or even, "Is CBT appropriate here?", but "Can you develop a CBT course for us?" Of course in many cases CBT is a solution to the problem, but in most cases it is not. But the company will rarely see it that way.

This tendency to go for fashionable 'solutions' is a particular danger when choosing a computer system. Especially when a businessman with little computer experience is receiving most of his 'advice' from a computer dealer or salesman.

You must address basic questions, and answer them honestly. Don't decide to get a computer and then investigate which one is best. First, decide what your needs are and then consider a computer as just one of the possible solutions.

If you have a business of any size, it is likely that you will be able to gain some benefit from using a computer. But even the largest businesses will find that they cannot rely solely on computer systems. So the problem is to identify the tasks where a computer will be useful, and to work out how the computer system will fit in with your manual procedures. This task of integrating manual and computer systems often produces major headaches for companies new to computers. This is because companies perceive computers as a solution to all their problems, and not a tool to be applied to do a specific job as part of an overall system. Because we have followed the method of looking at your business requirements as a whole, there is less danger of falling into this trap.

Now, we can expand our picture of the system as shown in Figure 6.1.

The computer system and the manual system must work together, exchanging information as needed. When systems pass information between each other, this is normally referred to as an interface. The arrows in figure 6.1 represent the interface between the manual and computer procedures.

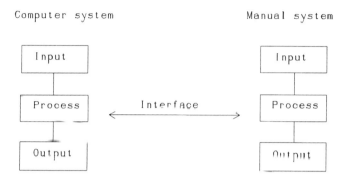

Figure 6.1

You should evaluate possible systems with this model in mind. Your eventual solution might be one of the following:

1. To keep an essentially manual system, but use software packages to speed up the most time consuming tasks (e.g. by using a database package to hold details of customers, and a spreadsheet to produce invoices and monthly reconciliations).
2. To computerize one of your main areas of activity (e.g. the sales ledger cycle), but otherwise use a manual system supplemented with utility software packages where appropriate.
3. To go for a fully integrated computer system, with only a few manual procedures used to handle tasks not suitable for computerization.

Many businesses go down the path of using an essentially manual system, with software packages used to carry out various individual tasks and reconciliations. This accounts for the great popularity of spreadsheet packages, which are ideal for autonomous tasks. Many large companies also follow a similar route, but instead of a manual system at the core, there is usually a mainframe system that cannot do what users need, so instead of enhancing the mainframe system, the users start using PCs to produce all their reports. It suits the needs of the user at the time, but leaves the long term DP strategy of the company in a mess.

The problem with developing a plethora of independent systems is that eventually, much effort is spent in shunting information from one system to another, often with the same information having to be typed in several times. And information in one of the systems cannot easily be linked to information in another. When you hear a computer consultant talk of 'interface problems', or 'integration problems', it is probably because a company has followed this route.

But the trap is easy to fall into. In the initial stages, you may be reluctant to commit the business to a full scale computerization, so you start by introducing a spreadsheet package to do some of the monthly reconciliations. When that works well, you decide to use a database system to hold your customer details. And then you decide to buy a payroll system to handle the wages. And so on, and so on.

So, while building a system piecemeal may produce some improvements, it is unlikely to be the best option for your business. In some instances you may decide consciously that an integrated system is not feasible, and that the only choice open to you is to computerize on a piecemeal basis around an essentially manual system. But think very carefully before you embark on this course. It is very rarely the best way to proceed.

But it *is* a feasible option to introduce the computer step by step: a modular approach is often successful. Using this method a system is gradually built up from several major chunks. But you must have an idea what the complete system is going to look like before you take the first step. And then each new system introduced is a building block towards a final integrated system.

Another advantage of the modular approach is that it gives you time. Once the first module is installed, there is no rush to install the second. So you can benefit from an extensive learning process before expanding the system.

There are two competing principles that apply to installing computer systems:

1. Achieve as much as possible within one single system, to minimize the effect of interface problems.
2. Always progress in small steps; in this way problems can be identified and resolved one by one. If you try to achieve too much in one leap, you are in danger of being swamped with all your problems at once.

If your proposed system consists of a number of properly integrated modules, you can come close to achieving both of these objectives.

But there are disadvantages to the modular approach. If you are employing someone to implement your system, it may prove expensive to retain a consultant's services over a lengthy implementation period. And while a step by step approach allows you to identify problems one by one, it does mean subjecting your business to a long period of continuous change. Some people might prefer to 'get it all over with' in one go. The demoralizing effect of constant change can be alleviated by taking a hefty breathing space between modules. But that means postponing the benefits of using the system...

And so the circle continues. But nobody said it was going to be easy.

If you decide that a modular approach is not the answer; either because the software doesn't allow that sort of approach, or because, for your business, the disadvantages outweigh the advantages; then you will be looking at a major 'one step' implementation.

There are two major problems to a one step implementation.

1. All the things that can go wrong, will go wrong together.
2. People using the system will have to surmount a huge learning curve in one go.

These risks can be minimized by meticulous planning and preparation for the implementation, and close attention to training procedures. (These are important, whatever course you take, but they assume an overwhelming importance when all your eggs are in one basket.)

The advantages of a one step implementation, are the converse of the disadvantages for the modular approach. There is no prolonged period of change, and the benefits of using the system are realized quickly.

When you consider these options, bear in mind that using a computer system will in itself create additional manual procedures. Often, the introduction of a computer system will cause a reduction in the number of clerical staff required. But in many cases staff requirements will stay level, or even increase. Many of the 'interesting' jobs will be replaced by the boring task of data entry, and this may have an effect upon morale. This can be turned to your advantage if you are able to liberate your more capable staff from routine work and allow them to spend time creatively, looking for business opportunities, providing a better customer service, and thinking about ways to improve things. But then you will have to employ people to carry out the data entry jobs, which will result in an increase in costs (but this may be justified if the business benefits overall).

Once you are aware of the strategic implications, you can start designing your system.

Detailed system design

The first stage in detailed system design, is to identify areas of the business where a computer system is unlikely to be a feasible solution. This can save you much time and heartache later on. Signs that a task is not suitable for a computer are:

> The volume of data involved is very small
> Little formal calculation is involved
> The task depends on subjective judgement
> Interpersonal skills are important
> Communication with the outside world is involved
> Interactive contact is important

For example:

> A construction company building a dam may use a project management system to schedule activities, but an experienced house builder could more efficiently plan out a job on the 'back of an envelope' - the data involved is too small to justify computerization.
>
> Or, a computer based training package might be the best way for an international organization to teach thousands of employees accounting procedures, but a similar course on sales technique would be a disaster - people skills are involved, and the opportunity for interaction with the teacher, and role playing exercises is important.

Once you have identified those areas where a computer is inappropriate, you can set about designing your system. Your aims should be:

1. All data coming into the system should be entered once and only once.
2. Data which is already known to the system should not have to be entered again (for example, if a suppliers address is required for an invoice or a purchase order, it should be called up automatically).
3. All output which can be standardized should be produced automatically by the system (for example, all purchase orders, invoices, statements, follow-up letters).
4. All calculations should be performed by the system.
5. All filing and retrieval should be electronic and automatic.
6. All data should be available quickly and easily.

7. Any task which is trivial and time consuming should be performed by the computer (e.g. production of labels for envelopes).
8. All periodic tasks, follow-up reminders, should take place automatically (e.g. reviewing overdue accounts, updating ledgers).

It is highly unlikely that you will achieve all of these aims. But the closer that you come the achieving them, the more benefit you will gain from your new system.

The extent to which you realize your aims will depend on how much integration you can build in to the system.

How do you start the design? In the early days of computer systems, there were two major stages: design the system, and write the software. However, with the advent of cheap commercial software packages, a different approach is needed. Now, your first task is to look at software packages that might provide a solution to some, or most, of your needs. Compare the packages available with the functions required by your logical model. Look for the fewest number of packages that can carry out the largest number of tasks. In effect, mentally carve up your logical model into a few big chunks, and match these chunks against an available package.

There may be gaps that you cannot fill easily, these will be taken care of by manual procedures, or use of utility packages (your 'interface' areas). If there are large chunks that you cannot find a package for, an alternative might be to build your own system, or subsystem using a 4th generation language (4GL).

Let's go back to our example company, the interior design consultancy, to see how this process might work in practice. What major areas of activity did we identify in our logical model? Looking at Figures 3.9(a) and 3.9(b), several threads stand out. In addition, we must account for dealing with correspondence, and purchase and maintenance of fixed assets (capital expenditure), which were not included in Figure 3.9. Table 6.1 shows a list of the major business activities together with possible software solutions.

Our aim is to build a system with as few interfaces as possible, within acceptable limits of cost, time, and disruption. Given large cost and time limits, we could build a tailor made system using only a database (with 4GL) and a cadd package. But this course requires a heavy investment, and carries the risk of an 'eggs in one basket' solution.

Another solution might be to take care of all the accounting functions (sales, stock, purchases, cash book, general ledger, fixed assets, and payroll) with a quality accounting package, and integrated payroll system. A database system would take care of the customer information file, progress reporting, and materials register. A cadd package, with possibly an art package, should take care of the designers' requirements. And a word processor will take care of correspondence and proposals. Preparing estimates could be done on a spreadsheet (as we demonstrated in the example in Chapter 4), but as it is the only spreadsheet application we have identified, it would save money if we could deal with it in another way. Modern word processors support simple calculations, and, as the list of needs (Figure 3.1) established 'Lay out documents professionally' as a prime requirement, a top class word processor is likely to be needed anyway. If a word processor solution is not feasible, it may be more cost effective to treat it as a manual procedure on a 'volumes of data' basis.

Once you have a strategy for building your system, it is time to start looking at the software and hardware products available.

Choosing Software

Where do you look to find out what software is available? We have already covered many of the major packages in chapter four (see also the reviews in Appendix C). But it is always a good idea to look at the most up to date information (especially in such a fast moving market). And there may be packages available specifically tailored to the needs of your type of business. The best sources for finding out about software packages are:

1. Computer magazines
2. Your trade journals (especially if you are in an unusual business).

At the end of Chapter 3 we discussed the constraints that governed whether micro-computers could (either singly or linked as a network) be a suitable hardware platform. But, as yet, we have not considered what particular make or model your system will run on. And there is good reason for this, a presumption that you will use a particular computer immediately puts restrictions on what software you can use. The driving sequence is: needs→software→hardware. Take full advantage of this flexibility, and look at the packages available across a wide range of machines. If you have an unusual requirement, there may be software available on a machine outside the normal business range. For example, if you require animation and music capabilities, an Amiga 2500 could be a better overall choice than an IBM-compatible PC.

Table 6.1

Business activity	Possible software solution
Keeping up to date records on everything going on for each customer	Database
Monitoring progress on jobs	Database
Producing design schemes	Art or Cadd package
Producing detailed designs	Cadd
Maintaining materials register	Database
Preparing job estimates	Database, spreadsheet, or word processor with maths
Accounting for sales	Spreadsheet or accounting package
Maintaining and accounting for stock	Database, spreadsheet, or accounting package
Accounting for purchases (materials and work sub-contracted)	Spreadsheet or accounting package
Maintaining the cash books and general ledger	Spreadsheet or accounting package
Maintaining the payroll	Payroll system
Dealing with correspondence and proposals	Word processor
Accounting for fixed assets	Spreadsheet or accounting package

Do not wander into a computer store and ask a salesman. That is the quickest and easiest way to squander money on useless hardware and software.

Once you have reviewed the available packages, you should have a fairly clear idea about whether any of them is likely to be of use. If so, draw up a short list and look at each package in detail.

There are criteria that any package you buy must fulfil.

1. It must be able to handle the volumes of data that you have identified as your system requirement (for example, number of suppliers, number of sales per day, etc.).
2. It must be able to handle the size of figures that you have identified in your specification for input and output documents (for example, if you specify that a suppliers balance can be up to 999,999, there is no point in buying a system that can only cope with balances up to 99,999).
3. It must have a close correspondence to your input and output requirements, and you must have thought of an alternative method of dealing with requirements that the package does not meet.
4. It must calculate any algorithms needed according to your specification.
5. It must produce output that conforms with statutory requirements (this can be very important if you have to make regular returns conforming to strict requirements, for example, VAT in the EEC, sales tax in the USA).
6. If you plan to feed information automatically into another system, it must produce a file in a format which the other system can read (or vice versa, if the package will be receiving information).
7. If your eventual system will run over a Local Area Network (LAN), the software must be available in a network specific version (or at least be capable of running over a network without causing problems).

You should carry out this exercise for each business area where a software package is required. Once you have a shortlist for each area, you can start thinking about hardware.

Your aim is to identify the software-hardware combination that best meets the needs of the business. Often, it is a good idea to standardize on a common hardware base. Using the same hardware for all applications cuts down on training costs, facilitates the transfer of data between applications, and gives flexibility to spread the processing load between machines.

But in some cases there may be good reasons for using different hardware for different tasks. If a particular machine is far superior to

its competitors in one specialized area, but lacks the flexibility to
satisfy your mainstream processing requirements, then it makes sense
to use the appropriate machine for the specialized task.

Once you have reviewed the various software-hardware combinations,
you can draw up a table, like that shown in Figure 6.2

Hardware	Software requirements				
	Word Processor	Database	Accounts Package	Art Package	Cadd Package
Apple Mac					
IBM AT comp.					
Amiga 2500					
Archimedes					

Figure 6.2

Across the top of the table enter the categories of software package
that you require, and enter the corresponding range of hardware down
the side. When you have drawn up the table, enter the software
packages on your shortlist in the appropriate boxes. If a hardware item
has at least one entry in each of the software categories, it represents
a possible solution.

At this stage, you can remove from your list, all software-hardware
combinations that do not form part of a complete solution.

Having established what software meets your base requirements, you
can undertake a more considered evaluation of the contenders in each
category. Questions that you should ask about each package are:

1. Number of useful features (sometimes called 'functionality').
   Useful is the important word here. An in-depth review in a good
   magazine often provides a good guide.
2. Speed. A fast package allows more work do be done in a shorter
   time, and allows resources to be released for other tasks. Look
   for 'benchmark' tests in magazines.
3. Additional hardware requirements. Does the package require
   additional memory, to run efficiently? Or does the package
   consume a lot more disk space than its competitors, with no
   corresponding increase in performance?

4. Ease of use. Will training be straightforward? Does it offer help for new users, and 'short cuts' for experienced users.

5. What is the manual like? A package with great features is of little use if you cannot find out what they are, or how to use them. And when you look at manuals, remember that an experienced user does not want to wade through pages of eloquent explanation, a short, easy to find answer saves time and frustration.

6. Integration. Is it easy to build bridges between the package and your other software choices? Most good software provides this capability, usually referred to as **import** and **export** of data.

7. On software that will be running over LANs, does it have efficient procedures for protecting the integrity of data in shared files? If a file is locked completely by the first person that wants to use it, then no further persons can access the data (this procedure is called **file locking**). However, good software uses **record locking** so that only one record at a time is unavailable to a second user.

When you have completed evaluating all the software candidates for your system, a preferred hardware category and software choice will become apparent. (It is not necessary to define a precise hardware configuration at this stage.)

Any decisions you reach will be provisional. The real test for a software package will come when you try to build your physical model by fitting the various packages together. You may then have to reconsider some of the software candidates.

It is likely that in most cases, you will be looking at a solution based around using one or more IBM compatible PCs. However, if you should find yourself fairly evenly balanced between a choice of hardware categories, the characteristics of the hardware itself might influence your decision.

If you are keen to promote ease of use, and reduce training times, the Apple range might be a good choice; if you want to produce high-tech presentations with integrated animation, video, and sound, then an Amiga could be considered. But if you want a reliable, business work horse with masses of available software, then an IBM compatible PC is a sensible choice.

But what if you cannot find a solution based around the available software packages? Or what if you can see your way to satisfying most of your requirements, but there is a gaping hole, where your business has specialized requirements? You may want to develop your own system.

Developing Your Own System

There was a time when developing a business system was a long, expensive business. The system had to be specified meticulously in advance, and a team of programmers would spend months, writing, testing, and debugging programs, probably writing the system in COBOL. Once the system was produced, making a minor change was a big task. Requests for system changes from users built into long backlogs, and often the waiting time for a simple amendment was over two years. Writing your own system was very much a game for the big boys.

But in recent years there have been significant changes. Using Fourth Generation Languages (4GLs), systems can be developed quickly, and changes can be made at will. So it is now often a feasible option for a small business to consider developing its own system. At the top end of the market, products such as **Oracle** and **Artemis**, are rich in features, but these may not be required by the small businessman, so it is doubtful whether they represent value for money. In the middle of the market, products such as **Dbase** and **Rbase** hold a large share. Dbase has become cumbersome in its later versions, with a clumsy SQL interface (see review in Appendix C), but on the other hand it is a widely known product in both the UK and US market place (Rbase, which on paper looks a better product than Dbase, is a long established product in the US). It is possible to buy a 4GL package at ever lower prices. The Dbase clones **Clipper**, and **Foxbase**, offer similar functionality to Dbase (sometimes better) at a cheaper price, while Megatech's **TAS+** offers superb value for money, with power features at a very cheap price (for the base level software, however 'bells & whistles' versions come a lot dearer. Megatech also offer a complete multi-user accounting system that can be run over a network, together with the source code: enabling you to customize and expand the system to suit your business.)

If you do decide to write your own system, you should employ a consultant. It is essential that someone in the business gets involved with the development of the system, and gets to know the 4GL that the system is written in. The main reason for this, is to make sure that the consultant understands your needs properly, and is producing a system that meets your expectations. By getting to know the 4GL you will gain independence, and eventually be able to modify your system as needs change.

A Software Choice for Our Example Company

What sort of packages would suit our interior design company? Let's propose two options (both assume IBM compatible PCs will form the hardware base).

Option one: All functions except design and document preparation will be catered for by a system written in-house using the **Tas+** multi-user accounting system (which includes the Tas 4GL language, together with the accounting system source code). The accounting system will be extended to include a materials register and a customer information facility. Document preparation and estimating will be done using **Wordperfect 5**. Designers will be asked to evaluate **Generic Cadd level 3, FastCad**, and **Autocad** for design work (**Gem Artline, Correl Draw**, or **Adobe illustrator**, could be considered for design schemes, should a cadd package prove unsuitable).

Option two: The customer information file and materials register will be set up using **Dataease**. The accounting system will be Sage's **Financial controller**, supplemented with the Sage **Payroll II** program. Document preparation and design activities will be dealt with as in option one.

Option one has the advantage of providing a high level of integration, together with the ability to expand and modify the system as the company grows and needs change. However, implementing the system will take longer and cost significantly more than option two. The most significant cost of option one will probably be the consultancy time required to design and implement the system (several weeks in consultancy fees at between £2,000-£4,000 a week). Option one will also require more staff involvement than option two, and consequently cause more disruption to the business.

Option two has been geared towards a fast, trouble-free implementation. The software products chosen (Dataease and Financial controller) are both easy to use, and can be installed quickly. Although option two will be a lot easier to implement than option one, the system produced will not be as efficient. No natural link will exist between the stock system and the materials register, neither will there be a link between the customer information file and the sales ledger. Additional manual procedures will be necessary to keep the various systems in step. An investigation into the most efficient way of interfacing the accounts and database system will need to be carried out.

In practice, you would decide between these options at this stage. But for example purposes, we will keep both options open for the time being.

Developing a Physical System Model

Your goals during this stage are to:

1. Make a final decision on your software/hardware requirements.
2. Produce a detailed specification for the physical system.

In order to make a final decision on your software and hardware requirements, you need to:

1. Confirm that all of your requirements have been covered.
2. Confirm that all the interfaces have been properly defined.
3. Establish what manual procedures are required.
4. Check that the selected hardware has the capacity to handle your processing and data storage requirements for the foreseeable future. (You should already have confirmed that PCs represent a feasible solution, following the guidelines we discussed at the end of Chapter 3.)
5. Specify the required hardware configuration. This is especially important if a local area network or multi-user solution is proposed.

The best way to start is to draw an overview diagram of your physical system. The diagram of the physical system will be based on the logical diagram of the system (which we developed in Chapter 3). But in the physical diagram, it is physical constraints and procedures that are highlighted. In the logical diagram, we decided how the information must flow. In the physical system description, we decide how that information flow should be handled.

Before we launch into a full overview, let's reconsider our ideas about systems from a more practical point of view. In Chapter 3 we said that any system can be thought of as input→process→output. But most systems do not function automatically. Manual intervention is required to input information, specify what processes are going to be performed, control when output is produced. So we can expand our picture of a system to look more like that in Figure 6.3. A practical example of how this might work with a payroll system is shown in Figure 6.4.

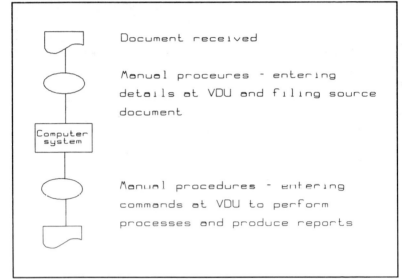

Figure 6.3

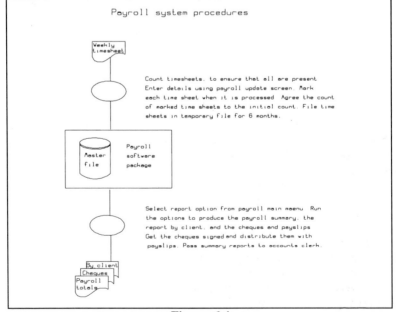

Figure 6.4

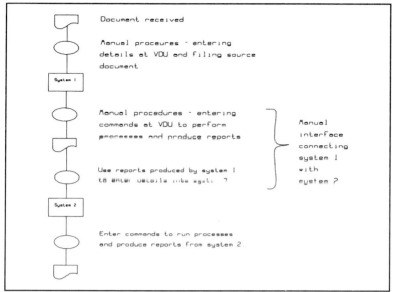

Figure 6.5

In most business environments there will be several systems operating, probably a mixture of manual and computer systems. Each of these systems may be thought of simply as input→process→output. But these systems will need to communicate with each other, i.e. they must **interface**. If you think about it logically, there is only one way that one system can interface with another; an output from one system will be the input for another. The interface may take place as an internal data transfer within the machine, or be a case of entering information from a report produced by one system using an input screen for another system. Whichever method is used, some form of manual procedure will be necessary for the transfer of information to take place. This is illustrated in Figure 6.5. The practical example shown in Figure 6.6 is an extension of the example shown in Figure 6.4. In this case output produced by the payroll system is used as input for two other systems.

The best way to get a full picture of how the components of your system interface with each other, is to draw an overview diagram. The overview diagram will be based on your logical system model.

An overview diagram for our example company, the interior design consultancy, is shown in Figure 6.7. In this diagram all manual procedures are represented by ellipses. A description of the first of

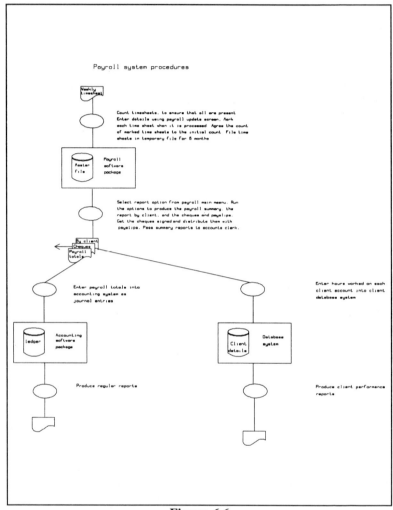

Figure 6.6

these procedures is shown in Figure 6.8. You should write a short description of all the procedures on your first overview diagram. Thinking through the system at this level of detail is an excellent way of highlighting any practical difficulties that are likely to arise. Compare the physical system overview in Figure 6.7 with the logical model we developed in Figures 3.8(a) and 3.8(b). Note how the logical model has been developed into a physical model.

In the case of our example company, the way that procedures are carried out will depend on whether option one or option two of our software choice is selected. Using option one, there will be few problems with interfacing. System efficiency will be determined largely by the structure of the 4GL code. But with option two, manual procedures will play a much larger part, and more thought needs to go into the high level design. For example, the accounting package (Financial controller) can produce output in the form of an ASCII file, but it cannot accept input in this way. The Dataease package, however can both read and write ASCII files. What is the significance of this? Consider a situation where new customer details are received. If they are entered first into the database package, then the only way to get the details into the accounting package is to type them in again. But if details are entered first into the accounting system, then a file can be produced, enabling the details to be transferred to the database system without re-typing. For a single enquiry, you may think that procedures for producing the file and reading it into the database system would probably take longer than re-typing the data. But when you consider that almost all the sales ledger data has to be passed to the customer information file, it soon becomes apparent that the introduction of transfer procedures will produce significant time savings. When you step through your overview diagram, making notes of the required manual procedures, these are the sort of things you should be looking for.

In tandem with producing a physical system overview, you should also sketch out a hardware configuration. (If your business will only need one PC, this may seem like an irrelevant exercise. But healthy businesses grow, and your requirements will expand quicker than you think!) Think about the numbers of people that will use each part of your system. If more than one person will need continuous access to the same part of the system, you may be looking at either a local area network or a multi-user solution (you should already have identified this possibility at the end of the 'Assessing your needs' stage). Let's take a closer look at how you decide what configuration is required.

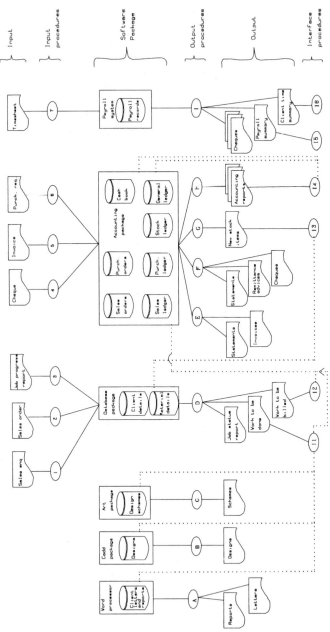

Figure 6.7

Key to Figure 6.7 - procedure 1

Input procedures

1. Once an enquiry is received, the customer enquiry screen is used to search for any existing records for that customer. If no record is found, the customer is allocated a 5 digit alphanumeric code (similar to the customer's name), a consultant is assigned to the customer (through 'phone call to manager), and the following information entered on the customer enquiry screen:
    Customer code (ends 'd' or 'c' for domestic or commercial)
    Name & Address
    Enquiry date
    Consultant
Correspondence is filed alphabetically in the customer correspondence file (archived after 1 year).

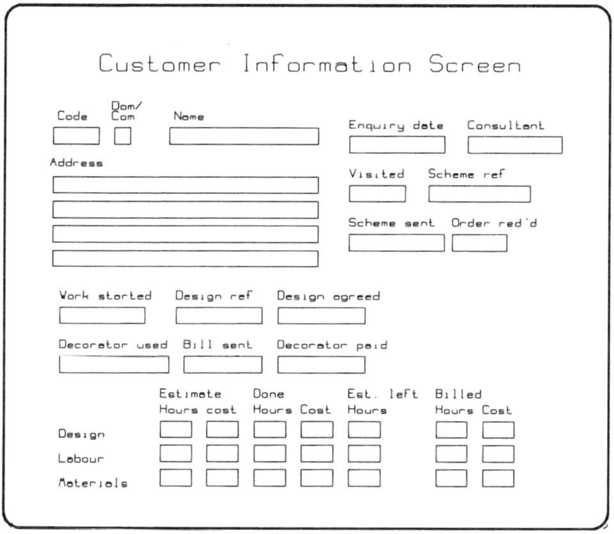

Figure 6.8

Deciding upon a Hardware Configuration

The performance of your system will depend, to a large extent, on how you organize your hardware and software. And the most efficient configuration for your system, will be dictated by how your system users need to share data. There are three major ways to configure a computer system.

1. A central computer handles all the processing and disk storage. Each user access the computer through a terminal. This is the 'traditional' configuration and is widely used for mainframe based systems.

2. A central computer handles all the disk storage, but the processing is shared over several processors (processors are the 'chips' that carry out all the work, see Chapter 2). This configuration is called **distributed processing**. In minicomputer, or mainframe environments tasks are allocated to processors by the operating system. But in a PC based system, a much simpler form of distributed processing is possible. Instead of a terminal, each user has a personal computer used to carry out all that user's processing.

3. Under the third option, not only is the processing distributed, but file storage is also spread across the computer network. A further development of this idea, is a system that holds a single, shared database, spread over several locations. This is called a **distributed database** configuration.

Option one is usually referred to as a **multi-user** system. Options two and three, are solutions based around **networks**. Let's consider each of these in more detail.

The Central Computer Configuration

Before personal computers became fashionable, the only common configuration for a computer system was that of a central computer serving many users, who would gain access via terminals (Figure 6.9). Often, most of the users would be using the computer to access one central database. For example, a large insurance company specializing in house insurance, may employ many clerks, all requiring access to a database containing policy details.

When many users share common data, it is inevitable that a large amount of information is travelling through the system at any one time. For the system to run efficiently, this traffic must be properly controlled, so it makes sense to design a system centred around a single, co-ordinating processor. Another requirement in a system of

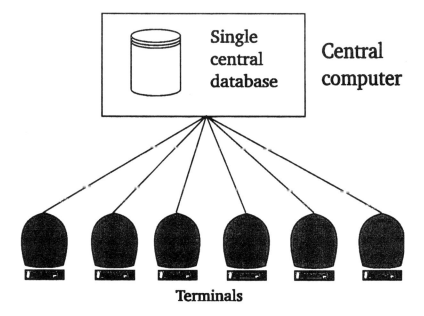

Terminals

Figure 6.9

this type, is to make sure that two users do not try and update the same record at the same time. Why? If one user updates a record while another user is working on the same record, the changes made by the first user, will be overwritten by the second user. Keeping to our present theme of insurance companies, an example of this is shown in Figure 6.10 (the consequence in this instance, is that the claim would be sent to the wrong address). The best solution to this problem, is to maintain central control of the database, allowing users access to only those records which are not currently being worked on. This type of control is achieved by using a type of software program called a Database Management System (DBMS). A single powerful processor, combined with fast disks, and a good DBMS is the most efficient way to share a database among many users.

Although this arrangement has, historically, been typical of a mainframe or minicomputer system, it can be implemented on a smaller scale using a 80386 based PC running a multi-user operating system (such as Concurrent DOS, or Unix). This arrangement will often prove best, in circumstances where several users need simultaneous access to the same database.

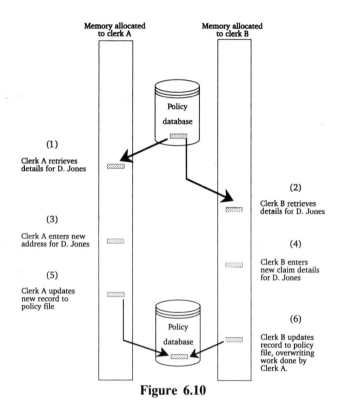

Figure 6.10

However, in some instances, users of the computer system would not all require access to the same data. Consider another insurance company, this time with a more diverse spread of business. This second company has a small operation in the areas of life, property, motor, fire, and commercial insurance. For the purposes of example, we shall assume that none of these business areas are related in any way, and that each branch of the business has its own separate database, maintained by one clerk. A business like this may use a system similar to that shown in Figure 6.11

In this instance, users do not need to share data. But because the system is controlled centrally, they will still have to wait their turn for the central processor to allocate them time, and give them access to disk files. In an environment where users are working on a number of different files, more time will be taken up as the processor moves from one disk drive to another, seeking out the files requested by the various users. And because terminal users have no disk storage of their own,

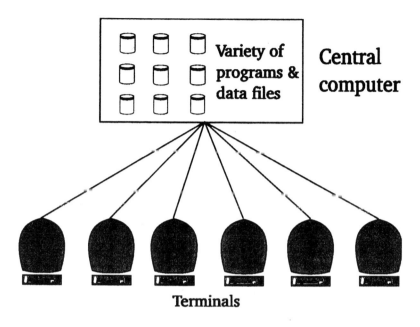

Figure 6.11

each time the processor moves from one user to another, information currently under review must either be held in memory (reducing the amount available for other users), or be written temporarily back to disk (slowing the system down).

Under these circumstances, it does not make sense to use the multi-user, central computer option. An alternative is to use a network.

The Distributed Processing Configuration

Using personal computers, a **distributed processing** configuration can be set up quite easily, using a Local Area network (LAN), as shown in Figure 6.12. The terminals have now been replaced by personal computers, and the central computer is now designated a 'File server'. Personal computers linked to networks are often referred to as **workstations**.

On a LAN of this type, all processing is carried out on the individual PCs, so that the only job the file server has is to feed data to users when it is requested. When a user wants to run a program, it is transferred across the network and loaded into the PC's memory. If a file is required, it is copied into the PC's memory. When work is

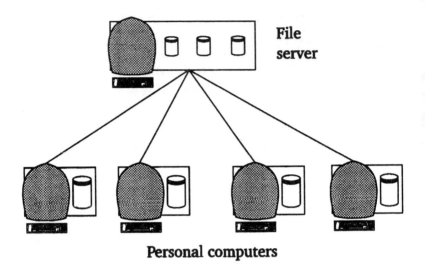

Figure 6.12

complete, the updated file is sent back over the network to the file server. This arrangement works well in circumstances where many users do not require access to the same file, and in cases where files worked on are small enough for the complete file to fit into memory at one time.

Many commonly-used LANs are built around the concept of a network driven by a file server. Under this arrangement, files held on the file server's disk, can be accessed by any machine on the network. But files held on another machine's disk, can be accessed by that machine only. Consequently, all shared files, must be held on the file server; even those accessed by other users infrequently. This arrangement degrades performance for the regular user of the file (who must always access it via the network), and causes an increase in the level of traffic, placing an extra burden on network performance generally. Some systems recognize this problem, and attempt to make disk access as efficient as possible (the Novell network system has specially written disk controller software, which bypasses the normal disk access routines).

But if most users work on their own data most of the time, there is a better alternative to a LAN based around a single file server.

The Distributed Storage Configuration

Under a distributed storage configuration, users can access data held on some (or all) of the individual machines in a network. To set up a system like this, you must either use a network that allows you to designate several of your PCs as file servers, or use a network that doesn't use a file server/workstation structure, but shares all resources equally (Figure 6.13).

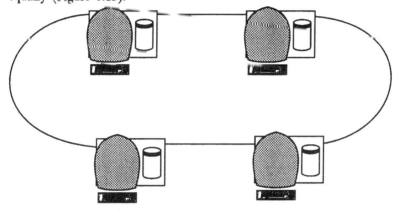

Networked PCs - no central server

Figure 6.13

Let's take an example where distributed storage would be beneficial. If a bought ledger clerk, and a sales ledger clerk are both using a system, it makes sense if the bought ledger files are kept on the bought ledger clerk's disk, and the sales ledger files are kept on the sales ledger clerk's disk. However, both clerks will require occasional access to information on the opposite ledger, and both ledgers must be available to a common system for consolidation at each month end. The ideal solution would be for the files to be stored on the appropriate clerk's disks, with both disks being accessible to a common network.

General Considerations on Networks

The development of networks has revolutionized the way PCs are used. Originally thought of as being handy 'utility' machines, in combination they can now provide cost effective solutions in circumstances where before, an expensive mini or mainframe computer was the only option. And because of the benefits of distributed processing, and distributed storage, the solution is often not only cheaper, but more efficient!

One of the stumbling blocks to the proper development of networking, has been the use of the file server/workstation design, which instead of solving the traditional mainframe problem of data management, has merely transported it to machines far less capable of handling high volumes of data. However, the approach to networking is slowly changing, and more systems are being developed with the goal of 'transparent' networking - a system whereby the physical location of a file or device is irrelevant to the operation of the network, enabling the benefits of distributed storage to be realized. (IBM is currently working on a transparent networking system to run under AIX - IBM's version of Unix.)

Choosing between a Network and a Multi-User System

How do you decide what hardware configuration is right for you?

1. If you have little, or infrequent requirement for users to share data, forget about networks, and use the time honoured method of passing a floppy disk.
2. If users need access to a large common database, look at a multi-user solution before networking. A 80386 PC running concurrent DOS can support 32 (relatively light) users on cheap, dumb terminals.
3. For heavy processing, with occasional data transfer, a network is the best choice (cadd, for example, is an obvious network application).
4. If users will be sharing a common program, but not common data, and working with small files, then networking can work well (for example, several users sharing a word processor).
4. If most network users have 'personal' data, use a network that doesn't insist on a file-server/workstation approach.
5. If you have a lots of light users (i.e. not using a lot of processing power), a multi-user solution can work out cheaper (dumb terminals are cheaper than PCs).

In general, multi-user systems perform better when a high degree of shared database access is needed, and LAN systems perform better when high processing capacity is required. Of course, most systems aren't so heavily biased towards one of these extremes that it is easy to make a decision. A good way to chose is to assess whether you have any applications that would rule out one system or the other. Let's go back to our example interior design company, and decide what configuration would be most suitable there.

Choosing a Hardware Configuration for the Example Company

In the company we have:

1. Four designers requiring machines with graphics capability
2. An office administrator requiring a machine to run the accounting system.
3. An office secretary requiring a word processor.
4. A general manager requiring information about the business.

The designers, office administrator, and secretary will all need full time access to a machine. The general manger will need only occasional access, but nevertheless, may wish to have a personal machine. Let's look at the requirements for each area in turn.

The four designers will run cadd software, possibly an art package, and a word processor, for producing letters and reports. It would be nice, but not essential, if all the design data and reports were stored centrally, for easy access. Cadd work is very heavy on processing power, but very light on disk access; a drawing is loaded at the beginning of a session, and saved at the end of it. Report and letter writing (for the designers) will place a negligible burden on the machine. The requirement for high processing power, with little disk access makes a network solution seem a reasonable proposition for the designers. But how will that fit in with the other requirements?

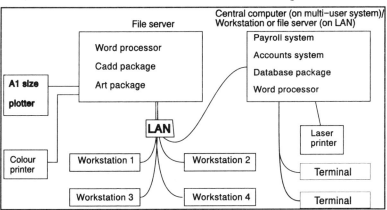

Figure 6.14

The office administrator will run the database software (for the materials register and customer information file), the accounting software, and possibly require occasional use of a word processor. However, only one of these jobs can run at a time, and none of them are likely to be heavy on the machine in terms of either processing requirements or disk access. The general manager will place a negligible load on the machine. On the face of it, the secretary will also place only a light burden on the machine. But what of the requirement in the list of needs, 'produce professionally laid out documents'? If this entails incorporating pictures and designs into brochures, the load on the machine can increase dramatically (graphics handling is always power hungry). But this requirement is likely to come only on the occasions when these documents are being prepared. The secretary will require a graphics screen (not colour) for desktop publishing applications. The administrator needs only a text based terminal. The general manager probably needs only a text based terminal, but may eventually wish to produce performance graphs and charts, so will probably insist on a personal computer with a colour graphics screen. Because the machine-load generated by the general manager, administrator, and secretary is generally low, a multi-user solution might be the best choice. However, it would be preferable if these machines were linked to the designer's machines, and these machines look as if they should run on a LAN. One option would be to run machines for the administrator, secretary, and general manager under concurrent DOS, and link these to a LAN for the designers. But, if a LAN is to be installed anyway, why not extend it to cover all requirements? Arguments could be made either way.

Would you consider running the whole system under a multi-user configuration? If the designers will be exerting a heavy processing load simultaneously, a single processor would crumble under the strain, so this option can be ruled out. So the two possible solutions are:

1. A Multi-user based system for the administrator, secretary, and general manager, linked to a LAN running for the designers.
2. One LAN serving all requirements.

These two options are illustrated in Figures 6.14 and 6.15. Under the first option, a PC acting as a file server supports the four designers on workstations one to four, and another computer acts as a central computer to the multi-user system, supporting the administrator, secretary, and general manager. The central computer on the multi-user system will also be set up as either a workstation, or file server on the LAN (depending on access requirements, and the capabilities of the LAN used). There are two points worth noting about this arrangement.

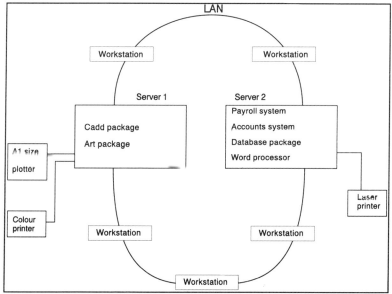

Figure 6.15

1. The designers' machines use a dedicated file server (using a single PC to act as a LAN file server and the core of a multi-user system would be risking too much, especially in the event of a failure).

2. Two terminals under the multi-user system require graphics capabilities (the secretary's and the general manager's). A system supporting graphics terminals is therefore required.

The advantage of this set-up is that terminals are cheaper than workstations, and the multi-user side of the system could be expanded at relatively low cost.

If the second option is chosen (Figure 6.15), the system is set up as a LAN with two file servers. Using this arrangement, one of the file servers could double up as the general manager's personal machine (which will be subject to only light use). The office administrator will use the other file server as a personal machine, as most of the files required by the administrator are on this machine, thus cutting down on network traffic. As six of the seven machines in the network require graphics capabilities, anyway, it might be prudent to specify that all are graphics machines, enabling users to switch between machines in the event of a failure (however, the designers may need to use enlarged screens).

For the interior design consultancy, using a single LAN system is probably the best solution. Combining a multi-user set-up with a LAN is over-complicated for a small company, serving only to increase the number of things that can go wrong. Also, a dedicated file server was required under the first option, whereas the file server doubles up as the general manager's machine under option two, reducing the total number of workstations/terminals required from eight to seven. So we will proceed on the basis that the company uses the configuration outlined in Figure 6.15.

One area we have almost ignored up until this stage is the use of output devices. The designers will need to produce artistic schemes and detailed designs. A colour printer will produce good results for schemes (intended to impress prospective clients), but a plotter will be required for the size and detail requirements of designs. If the secretary is to produce impressive proposals and reports, a laser printer will be needed to achieve quality output. These peripherals have already been included in Figure 6.15.

Once you have decided upon your hardware configuration, you must choose network software and hardware (netware) that meets your requirements. Before you do this, you should read all recent reviews and read at least one book on the subject. Here are four of the key questions you should ask:

1. Does the system insist on a dedicated file server?
2. Can any workstation in a network access the resources (disks and printers) of any other workstation?
3. Does the network support multiple file servers?
4. Does the networking software leave enough free memory for you existing applications to run? (Don't overlook this one.)

Asking these questions might stop you from being caught out, but there are a host of other considerations (such as security features and e-mail support) that you should read about before investing in netware. For our example interior design company, we have relatively modest requirements. But it is essential that the network supports multiple file servers. Sage's Mainlan system satisfies this requirement and represents a good choice of network for our example company.

The last stage in defining your hardware configuration is to specify the performance requirements of each machine.

The Server 1 machine (in Figure 6.15) will hold the cadd and art software packages, schemes, and detailed designs for all clients. This machine will also serve as the general managers personal machine. To act as a server, a reasonable amount of power is required, but the amount of disk access required should not be too great, so an AT compatible based on a 80286 processor, running at 12 or 20 Mhz should suffice (a Dell 220 might be a good choice). The machine should have a hard disk of several hundred megabytes, as graphics files tend to consume a lot of space (use of the DOS 4 or DR-DOS operating systems would allow disk partitions greater than 32 megabytes). The four designer's workstations will require plenty of power for the graphics processing and high-resolution, colour screens, but they will not need hard disks. So we are thinking in terms of 80386 based machines running at 25 or 33 Mhz, with at least VGA standard monitors, or perhaps a requirement for specialized large monitors.

The Server 2 Machine (Figure 6.15) will be used for all the accounting, database and word processing work. Again, a 20 Mhz 80286 machine would suffice, with a hard disk capacity of about a hundred megabytes. A machine of similar power with no hard disk would be suitable for the secretary (for normal word processing work a machine with a lower specification would be sufficient, but power is required for the desktop publishing applications).

Before we finalize the hardware configuration for the example company, we should perform some graphics benchmarks on some high power machines (to ascertain the best model for the job), discuss monitor requirements with designers, and ascertain more precisely the role and future requirements of the general manager (which in the real world, might be you).

Finalizing the Specification

Once you have created a physical system overview diagram, and established a hardware configuration, you will have a clear picture of the shape of the final system. As a consequence, you will be able to establish the likely cost of the hardware (but do not forget that training costs, and lost time are also significant). This is a good stage to look at the system from a 'value for money' or 'bangs per buck' point of view.

In the case of our example company, you might question whether the four designers need to use a LAN. Because they are each responsible for different clients, they do not need to access each other's data. If they did need access the easiest and cheapest way to get data from one computer to another is to walk across the office with a floppy disk. You might also question whether the general manger needs a PC. Abandoning the use of a LAN, together with the general manager's PC might reduce hardware costs considerably. And the option to upgrade to a LAN will still be there, as long as the software used at the outset can be upgraded to a LAN version. But this argument neglects the fact that using a LAN can actually save money. Under the LAN based system, only two of the seven machines used have hard disks. If a LAN was not used, all seven would need hard disks. This represents a considerable cost saving. Also, using the LAN, sharing printers is easy and convenient. If a LAN was not used, it may become necessary to buy individual printers.

When you are happy that the system in your mind is complete, viable, and cost effective, it is time to produce a detailed specification. This should contain:

1. A complete list of the inputs to the system, specifying in what form the information is received (e.g. from 'phone call, on disk, on paper). Example forms/screens should be included.
2. A description of the manual procedures required to load the information into the system.
3. Procedures for dealing with forms received once they have been processed.
4. Procedures required to instruct the system to carry out processing of information.
5. Procedures required to instruct the system to produce output.
6. A complete list of the output produced by the system, specifying in what form the information is produced (e.g. as a message on screen, on paper, on disk). Example screens, reports should be included.
7. Procedures for dealing with the output produced.
8. Segregation of each subsystem/package, with the information flow to and from each subsystem/package being clearly identified.
9. Procedures for passing information from one system to another.
10. Identification of major stores of information within each subsystem/package.
11. A detailed specification of all the hardware requirements.
12. In an environment where different types of hardware are being used, hardware used for each process must be separately identified.
13. Special input/output requirements should be identified (e.g. need for special printers/plotters for output, or bar code readers for input).
14. Periodic procedures (e.g. weekly reports, monthly accounts, debt-chasing routines).
15. An estimate of the hardware, software and maintenance costs.

When you have completed most of the work on your system specification, the *last* thing to write is the first section.

The first section of the system specification should contain a complete list of the objectives of the system implementation, together with a list of benefits that will be gained form the implementation. If you are the owner of your business, you may feel that this is a waste of time. Who are you trying to convince? But the objective of this section is not to 'sell' the system; that should have been done long before this stage. Because the system design is complete, you should now have a clear idea of what you want to achieve, and how it will help the business. By the time that the messy process of implementation is complete, you will have forgotten some of your objectives. By writing them down now, you will have a yardstick against which to measure your final system. Where possible, make your objectives precise, and measurable. If you think that time spent processing purchase orders can be reduced by 50%, then make that an objective; it is a figure that can be verified later. On the other hand, there are some equally important criteria, such as staff attitudes to the system, which can not be measured with any precision. But these should not be left out. You will just have to accept a less objective measure.

Theory and Practice

Although we have set out the stages of system development as steps in a logical sequence, in practice an iterative process is likely to occur. For example, it is only when you turn your attention to mapping out the procedures required to hold a system together, that you appreciate the overhead of maintaining manual interfaces between systems. This may prompt you to re-consider your original software choices, and try to find a more automated way of linking systems together.

Designing a system in practice is a lot messier than carrying out a theoretical exercise, so if you find yourself going around in circles, don't be dismayed! But a time will come when decisions have to be taken. You will never be perfectly happy with a proposed system. System development, in common with all other projects, has a tendency to become 90% complete quickly, and then progress no further. So don't prevaricate, when you have a viable system with a clear path for growth, freeze the specification, and start an implementation plan.

Summary of Chapter 6 - Designing the System

Strategy

Start with basic questions - Do I need a computer?
Avoid fashionable solutions - be driven by your needs.
Never trust a salesman!

Types of system:

Autonomous modules, built up piecemeal
Modular systems
Central manual system assisted by utilities
Single integrated system

Advantages of modular approach:

Achieves goal of final integrated system
Still allows the control of a step by step implementation

Disadvantages of modular approach:

Not always possible, if software not easily broken up
subjects business to prolonged period of change
Benefits not realized until implementation complete

Advantages of one-step implementation:

Single cohesive system guaranteed
Restricted period of change
Benefits realized quickly

Disadvantages of one-step implementation:

All problems hit you at once
Big learning curve for staff
Meticulous planning essential

Competing principles:

Achieve as much as possible within one single system, to
minimize the effect of interface problems.
Progress in small steps; in this way problems can be identified
and resolved one by one.

Implications of computerization for staff:

Often a requirement for new 'boring' data entry tasks
Time of senior staff released for more creative work
Often, numbers of clerical staff can be reduced

Detailed design

Identify jobs not suitable for computer:

The volume of data involved is very small
Little formal calculation is involved
The task depends on subjective judgement
Interpersonal skills are important
Communication with the outside world is involved
Interactive contact is important

System aims:

Data entered once and only once
Data already known to the system not entered again
All standard documents produced automatically
All calculations, filing and retrieval performed by the system
Data available quickly and easily
All trivial, time consuming tasks performed by computer
All periodic tasks, follow-up reminders take place automatically

In the past systems developed from scratch, the modern approach is to put together software packages that meet your needs.

Sources of software information:

Magazines
Trade journals

The driving sequence:

Needs→software→hardware

Base criteria for software:

Can handle data volumes
Can handle the size of figures required
Close correspondence to input and output requirements
Calculates algorithms according to requirements
Output conforms with statutory requirements
Can exchange data with other packages, where required
Supports LAN if LAN needed at present or possibly in future

Pick the hardware solution that best accommodates your software requirements.

Standardize on hardware if possible, but don't be afraid to use the correct machine for a specialized requirement.

Final selection criteria for software:

Number of useful features
Speed
Memory and disk requirements
Ease of use
Good manuals, including quick reference for experienced users
Integration with other packages
Satisfies file and record locking requirements for LAN based systems

Writing your own system:

Employ a consultant
Someone in the business should be closely involved, making sure that the system meets expectations, and acquiring the knowledge to modify the system as needs change

Finalizing your system model:

Draw an overview of the physical system
Draw a diagram of the hardware configuration

Write outline descriptions of all the manual procedures required; step through the system mentally, thinking of the staff involved, what they have to do, and whether the system is feasible.

Estimate hardware requirements:

Decide upon the right configuration - single machines, LAN, or multi-user
Carry out benchmark tests for hardware suitability
Resolve questions raised by your system overview, through consultations with staff

Produce a final, detailed specification for the system, including:

Inputs and outputs
Manual procedures
Complete hardware specification
Hardware and software identified with each subsystem/package
Information flow to and from each subsystem/package
Interface Procedures

Major information stores within each subsystem/package.
Special input/output requirements should be identified (e.g. need for Periodic procedures
Hardware, software and maintenance costings.

Theory and practice:

System development is an iterative, circular process
But:
Don't prevaricate unduly. When the time is right commit to implementation

CHAPTER 7

Implementing the System

Once you have a physical system designed on paper, you may feel that installing it is a formality. But implementation problems often produce as many headaches as all the other stages in the development process put together.

Several things need to be done:

1. Produce an implementation plan.
2. The system you have designed must be built and tested.
3. The data on your old system must be transferred to the new system.
4. Procedures for handling 'old' data not satisfying the requirements of the new system must be developed.
5. A smooth transition from one system to the other must be planned.
6. Staff need to be trained in how to use the new system.
7. Manuals for using the new system must be produced, or made available.
8. Existing documents which refer to the old system, must be updated.

The first thing that must be achieved is an implementation plan. As with the other stages of development, involving staff is important, particularly those who have a heavy involvement in the old system.

Strategy

There are two ways to implement a new system:

1. All at once.
2. Step by step.

There are several benefits to be gained from implementing a system in stages:

1. Problems can be encountered and dealt with one at a time.
2. Staff have time to become familiar with the hardware and learn to use the system.
3. If a disaster occurs, the damage is limited to those parts of the system that have been implemented.
4. Lessons learnt from the first stages of implementation can be incorporated into later stages.

Some systems cannot be implemented in easy stages. If a system is built around one major piece of software then it cannot be implemented step by step. But generally speaking, these systems are few and far between. Most systems can be broken down into a number of constituent parts. Although there are some advantages to a one step implementation (see the discussion in Chapter 6 on modular system design), if a company is new to computers, a step by step approach is to be highly recommended. When a computer first arrives, even the simplest of tasks (such as copying disks, and starting a program running) can cause difficulties. The implementation of a new system will run much more smoothly, if staff are already familiar with the machine.

To enable staff to become familiar with the machine, the first application introduced should be easy to learn, and relatively autonomous and unimportant (from a system point of view). Word processing is suited ideally to this purpose. In a department where several users are going to be using a computer for the same purpose, it is a good idea, if it is possible, to introduce the system as a 'pilot scheme' with a small number of users before a wholesale implementation. Feedback from a pilot group can be invaluable (so remember to ask for it!).

Once users are familiar with the machine, it is a good idea to introduce your 'core' applications: the parts that are central to the operation of the system. It is much easier to build your system around a solid core than it is to try and fit the core in later, when a number of peripheral systems are already established. Let the needs of the core system drive the development of the remainder.

Implementing a system in stages causes problems of its own. You may have designed procedures for handling the transfer of data from one part of a new system to another, but what about the mid-implementation stage, when one part of the system is in place, but the other is not? To be able to anticipate these problems, you must develop a clear implementation plan. For each stage of the implementation, you must decide:

1. The parts of the system that are to be implemented.
2. Procedures for testing the system, and making sure that the initial data is taken on correctly.
3. Special 'handover' procedures required over the implementation period.
4. Staff training requirements.
5. Documentation requirements.
6. How this stage affects subsequent stages of the implementation.

Management of the implementation can be made considerably easier by breaking down the overall plan into a few major, independent phases. If problems arise with one phase, more resources can then be diverted by delaying another phase.

A good way to represent your plan is in the form of a bar chart, showing the activities within each phase. (If an implementation is particularly complicated, it may be worth building a critical path network, but this would be going too far for most small system implementations.)

Let's develop an implementation plan for our example company, the interior design consultancy. The system we have designed can be broken down into the following modules:

1. Word processing
2. Accounting.
3. Payroll.
4. Materials information.
5. Customer information.
6. Detailed design.
8. Scheme production.

These modules can be grouped into three phases:

Phase one	Word processing and accounts
Phase two	Materials and customer information
Phase three	Schemes and designs

Each of these phases can be planned, and progressed independently. A barchart of the activities for phase one, and the first three activities of phase two is shown in Figure 7.1 (some of these activities will be explained in more detail later). Phase three is a separate exercise. A good way to introduce phase three would be to ask one designer to use a cadd system for a few months to iron out the problems before moving all the designers onto a cadd system.

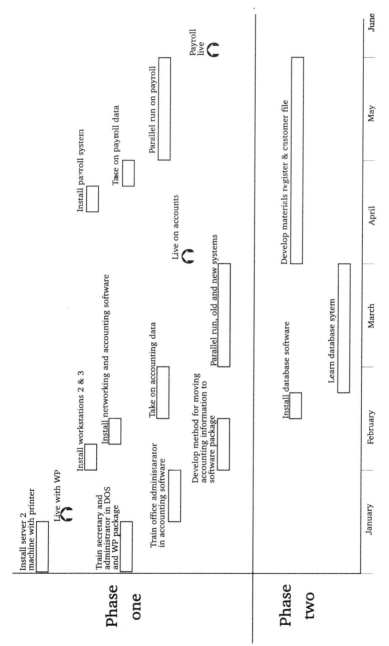

Figure 7.1

When you have a strategy for the implementation, it is time to look at the detailed problems.

Planning the Implementation in Detail

Before you reach that critical point where you switch from using one system to using another, it is essential that you have full confidence that the new system can take on the processing of the business. There are two basic strategies for achieving this:

1. Simulation. Load up the new system with test data, and carry out all the activities that will be required in normal business use. Check the results achieved by the system against the expected results (calculated manually).
2. Parallel run. For a normal business period, usually one week, or one month: run both systems. Check that the results obtained with the new system, agree with the results obtained with the old system.

Both of these approaches take up a lot of time and effort, especially the parallel run. But the consequences of not testing the system fully can be dire.

The best method is the parallel run. But in some circumstances it is not always possible, for example; when the new system represents such an advance on the old system that comparison is meaningless, or; when the resources required to do a full parallel run of the two systems are not available. However, if you possibly can go for a parallel run, you should do so.

One of the first practical problems you should attack, is the method of data transfer. If you are going for a parallel run, you will need to transfer all the old system data onto the new system before the parallel run can begin. If you are going for a simulation, then transferring all the data onto the system does not need to take place until just before you go 'live', but it is advisable to use existing data for your simulation, this will provide a realistic test of the system, and allow you to prove your data transfer procedures.

Make a list of all the information that is to be held in the new system, i.e., which **fields** are to be in which **file** held in which software package (see the section in Chapter 3 on databases for coverage of *fields* and *files*), and make a similar list for the old system (for non computer systems, the equivalent may be which box, on which card, in which filing cabinet). Check that all the information in the old system is to be accounted for in the new system. If information held in the old system is to be dispensed with, check carefully that this information is genuinely redundant. If information is required for the new system, that was not available under the old system, you have two choices:

1. Decide upon special arrangements for handling 'old system' data.
2. Manually input the required additional information into the new system.

Where information held under the old system is stored on computer (for example, accounting system information could be held in a spreadsheet package), look careful at the possibility of electronic transfer to the new system. Many software packages support import and export of data, using a variety of standard formats. The most basic method of transferring data is in a plain ASCII file. Data values are normally separated by commas and surrounded by quote marks to separate one field from the next; records are separated by a carriage return character. This type of data transfer is normally referred to as a **Flat file transfer** (some systems can also perform direct 'on-line' transfers, but this is unlikely to be an option in the case of a small business with limited computer exposure).

If no electronic means of transferring data is possible, you will have to make arrangements for manual transfer of data. Identify the reports/listings produced by the old system that will present the information in the most efficient way for updating through input screens in the new system.

Where the new system is made up of several interfacing modules, there is a good chance that a flat file transfer will be available to save you entering data twice. In our example interior design company, the stock information might be entered into the accounting system first, and, when phase two of the system is implemented, a flat file transfer made to load a list of all the stock items into the materials register in the database package.

Not only will you need to make arrangements for transferring data, but it should be checked thoroughly (regardless of whether it was transferred manually, or by flat file transfer). Decide which reports or listings will provide the best means of ensuring that data has been entered correctly (remember that one of these should come from the old system, and one from the new, otherwise the check is worthless). It is essential that the people who check that the data has been entered correctly are different from the people who entered the data. When you establish checking procedures, make full use of control totals, such as ledger balances. If the new system calculates the total ledger balance to be identical to that worked out manually on the old system, it will give you a great amount of confidence that the transfer has been carried out correctly.

When you have a plan for transferring the data, look at procedures for the parallel run (or simulation). Over this period, a great strain will be placed on your resources, as you are doubling your clerical effort by running two systems (one of which your staff hardly know), while at the same time carrying out checking procedures to make sure that the two systems are in step. Using a barchart for your implementation plan can be a great help when planning your manning requirements, as you can see at a glance all the activities that will be carried out at the same time.

At the end of the period of parallel running, you will need to check all of the old system output against results produced by the new system. Again, use of control totals is especially useful here. And conversely, if two accounting systems show a different trading profit over the month, you know one of them must be wrong! If possible, plan to use the same staff for checking the initial data transfer, and the results of parallel running, as they will have learnt from the first exercise.

Assume that the discrepancies will be found, and allow 48 hours to resolve them. It is almost inevitable that they will, and you cannot go live with the system until they are resolved. The alternative is a second month of parallel running.

If you are forced into carrying out a simulation, instead of a parallel run, it is a good idea to mirror at least some aspect of the business where possible. In this way you may be able to use sub-totals for departments, or areas of business, as a cross check against the old system.   Checking procedures should be especially prudent where a simulation is used.

Once you have a plan that is technically feasible, in that it seems possible to transfer the data, check it, and move smoothly onto the new system; you can add training and documentation to your plan.

Training

There will be a training requirement for:

1. Software packages used in the new system.
2. Any systems written specifically for the new system.
3. Manual procedures associated with the new system; filing of documents, interface procedures.
4. Procedures for implementing the new system.

The timing of the training will depend on what use you plan to make of your staff during the implementation period. If they are to be heavily involved in the data transfer, parallel running, and checking procedures, then they will need training in the new system in advance. But if they are not to be involved in the new system until it goes live, then early training will be largely wasted, as they will have forgotten much of the information by the time they have to apply it. It is likely that some of your staff will fall into the former category and some. into the latter, so the training timetable will need to be split to accommodate this.

Training requirements in the new system will also vary for staff from different areas and at different levels. In our example company, only the designers will require training on the CADD and art packages, and only the administrator will require training in the accounting system. The general manger will require an overview of all systems, but may not want in-depth knowledge of each.

Once you have established who needs what training and when, how do you go about providing it? There may be commercial courses available for some of the software packages you have bought, but you will have to develop your own training material for company specific issues, such as manual procedures, filing requirements, system interfaces, and implementation procedures.

The aims of your training programme should be:

1. To inform the staff of the general strategy behind the new system, explaining why it is of benefit to the company, and why it is of benefit *to them.*
2. To remind the staff that they have been consulted, and to demonstrate that their requirements have been taken into account and acted upon.
3. To give staff an overview of the new system showing how they will fit in, and emphasizing their importance to the system as a whole.
4. To give staff the necessary knowledge and skills to operate the new system effectively.

Many companies make the mistake of seeing the last point, but missing the first three. The most essential ingredient for the success of any new system is staff commitment and enthusiasm for it. The first three points all concentrate on this area.

Working from the list of general aims, you should be able to compile a more detailed list of training objectives.

The most effective way to train a topic will depend on the *type of learning* involved, and the type of learning involved will become apparent from your training objectives (pioneering work was done in this area by Benjamin Bloom who produced a taxonomy of learning, which underpins many modern training methods).

Conceptual high-level learning (synthesis and evaluation) requires more sophisticated training than lower order skills (analysis and application) which in turn require a greater training effort than the lowest level of learning (recall).

Techniques which are good for training higher order skills are interactive presentations, extensive use of diagrams and pictures, active involvement in case studies, and use of analogy. For learning to be effective, a structure must be placed up front, and then the constituent parts of that structure covered in turn. Higher order learning is at takes place most effectively when trainees can form patterns, and relate facts together; presenting a clear structure is an immense aid to this pattern forming process (the **Gestaltic** theory of learning).

So, to introduce staff to a new system a presentation is probably a good place to start. Structure the presentation carefully, and tell them the structure at the beginning of the presentation. Concentrate on strategy, go through an overview of the system, and spell out the benefits *to them*. Use slides with lots of pictures and diagrams, avoid slides with more than a minimum amount of text. Ask them questions regularly, and encourage them to ask you questions. At the end of the presentation go over the structure again, recapping on the main points you have covered[1].

For training in manual procedures, a workshop session is a good idea. Prepare some detailed notes on how the system is going to work, and put together some exercises using sample data. Bring the staff together, with all the necessary equipment, explain briefly how the system works, and them let them use it in practice, going through the exercises you have prepared.

Training in software packages can either be accomplished using an established commercial course, developing training yourself, or by relying on the manuals/tutorial packages that come with the software. Some packages do not demand the higher order learning skills usually associated with a full blown presentation, but, again, an informal practical workshop is often effective. When learning a practical subject, there is no substitute for trying out the real thing. Use of a self-study book with exercises to carry out is a good way to further reinforce this training (but an expert should be available to answer questions during self-study sessions).

If you find that you have a significant training requirement, it is a good idea to undertake a more detailed study of training technique, and

---

[1]*"How to Give a Successful Presentation*', available in this series by the same author, is a step by step guide to the process of preparing and giving a presentation.

consider employing the services of a training consultant. The importance of training is often under-estimated. Training is a one-off expense, but the benefits accrue for many years. However, many managers persist in holding the view that time spent in training is non-productive, and that training costs are avoidable, and hence should be avoided. Because the benefits of training (and conversely, the costs of not training) are not easily quantifiable it is difficult to justify training expenditure on a case by case basis, especially in companies that measure performance against the narrow yardstick of short term costs. However, the majority of successful companies do not measure performance on this basis, and spend significantly more than average on training (on a wider scale, the same can be said for economically successful countries). One way that the case can be made for training is as follows: if a company has spent, say, £25,000 on implementing a system, and nobody can use it properly, no improvement in performance can take place, and the investment has been wasted. However, if the company had been prepared to spend an additional £5,000 on training, staff would know exactly how to use the system, and significant benefits would result. It is clear from this that there are only two sensible strategies: either commit to spending the £30,000, and achieve all the possible benefits, or; spend nothing and get no benefits. To follow the middle course, spend £25,000 and still get no benefits seems ridiculous. But for many companies who have just forked out £25,000, the chance to 'save' the extra £5,000 is too tempting. Think first! Remember also that much of the training material developed for implementing the system can be used to train new staff for many years to come.

Documentation

The reasons why a system should be properly documented are almost too obvious to state. But here are some anyway:

1. If you do not have a permanent record of the way your system is to work, your whole system can fall apart when a key member of staff leaves.
2. If somebody forgets how a procedure should work, there must be some way of looking it up.
3. Staff training will need to be supported by adequate reference material.
4. Auditors coming into the company will need a description of how the system works.

In addition to documenting your normal operating procedures, if you intend to produce a bespoke system using a 4GL, then it is imperative that the system you produce is documented thoroughly; otherwise it become almost impossible to maintain and adapt (the consultant you employ to produce the system should be able to give you further guidance on this).

When you produce documentation, it is important to remember that you are addressing two separate audiences:

1. Those new to your system, who need to find out how it works from scratch.
2. Experienced users of the system, who have forgotten how to do something, and need to find out quickly.

For this reason, it is good to produce at least two documents for every system you intend to document. These two documents are often called a **User Guide**, and a **Reference Manual**.

Because the user guide assumes zero knowledge of the system, it should start from a general point of view, explain the concepts behind the system, give an overview of all the system functions, and gradually go through all the features of the system, showing how they inter-relate. Good user guides typically contain lots of explanatory diagrams, and use 'real life' examples to illustrate the procedures covered. A useful technique in preparing a user guide is to use a single 'case study' example that develops with the material covered (in a similar manner to the way we have used the example interior design company in this book). The structure of a user guide should follow the natural structure of the system being covered. Clear contents, and a good index add greatly to the usefulness of a user guide.

A reference manual is aimed at the experienced person in a hurry. A good index is vital. Economy of language, and extensive cross referencing are other essential ingredients. Think of the person who is rushing to finish a job and is suddenly held up through forgetting a simple procedure. Imagine how frustrating it is to go through pages of verbiage trying to locate the one single piece of information needed. Unfortunately, many reference manuals are written by technical authors who are keen to show how clever they are at making technical things easy to understand, and in doing this produce pages of eloquent description. Don't make this mistake. Remember, the reference guide is for somebody who already knows the system. Save the eloquence for the user guide.

When you produce your documentation, another tiresome task is to update references to the old system in other company documents. In a small company this is unlikely to be significant burden, but in a large company these sort of tasks can become a nightmare. If your company starts to grow rapidly, maintaining control over systems documentation is an area that you can't afford to forget.

Getting the Show on the Road

Once your plans for testing, going live, training, and documenting the system are in place, you can install the system, and go ahead with your plan.

Unpack and set up all hardware following the manufacturers instructions. Once software is installed, *immediately* start performing tests to check that the system performs as planned.

Once hardware and software is installed, use a small amount of test data to feed data into all the packages you are using, and try out all the features that you will need to use in practice. Interface procedures where you will linking one package with another are especially prone to hiccups, and you should pay special attention to these. If any problems arise, get in touch with the hardware/software vendors immediately, and find out where the problem lies.

If you have followed the methods outlined throughout this book, no insuperable problems should be encountered at this stage, but it is surprising how many quirks arise in practice. Don't wait until you are going through your implementation 'as planned' to iron these out.

If errors occur at any stage during your data transfer, simulation/parallel run, or, final implementation tests, *do not proceed with the implementation until the discrepancy has been dealt with, re-tested and confirmed as functioning correctly.*

Your resources will be heavily strained during the implementation period, so avoid taking on any unnecessary work, and give your staff as much support and encouragement as possible.

Once your system is live, you next task is to see that it is properly maintained and supported.

Summary of Chapter Seven - Implementing the System

Main tasks during implementation:

Produce an implementation plan
Build and test the system
Transfer data from old to new system
Develop procedures for handling 'old' data
Move from old to new system
Train staff
Produce documentation

Strategy:

> Break down the system into modules, and implement in stages, where possible
> Group modules into major phases, for better management of implementation
> Use barcharts to set out your implementation plan

Detailed planning:

> Two common strategies for testing a new system:
>> Simulation - a test of the new system using selected data
>> Parallel run - running both systems in parallel over a period
> Make complete lists of old system and new system data, and decide the most efficient way to transfer between systems
> Ensure that data not transferred is genuinely redundant
> Decide whether special procedures will be needed for information required by new system, not present in old data
> Utilize **flat file transfer** techniques if appropriate
> Data transferred must be independently checked, making full use of control totals
> At the end of the parallel run/simulation a second check will confirm that the system is running correctly

Training:

> Required for Software packages, systems written internally, manual procedures, implementation procedures
> Different people will have different training needs
> Timing of training will be affected by your implementation plan
> Different training techniques are required for different types of learning
> Staff should be told strategy behind the new system, given an overview, and be reassured that their needs have been taken into account
> Use a presentation for outlining strategy, giving overview of system
> Use workshop sessions for manual procedures/software training
> Self-study exercise are good reinforcement for software training
> Consider using commercial courses for software training (especially if there is a high conceptual content)
> Training is cost effective!

Documentation:

Is necessary to protect against staff taking knowledge with them, as a reference, to support training, and to provide information to auditors.
A user guide should be produced for new system users, and a reference manual for experienced users.

Getting the show on the road:

Test all software/hardware for faults as soon as it is received
Avoid taking on unnecessary work during the implementation period
Support your staff

CHAPTER 8

Maintaining the System

Once your system is installed and up and running, you may think that your problems are over. But is easy to snatch defeat from the jaws of victory at this stage by forgetting to take a few simple precautions. The most important areas to think about are:

1. Is the system fulfilling the functions intended?
2. Is the system working according to specification?
3. Are the users aware of all the features available, and using them efficiently?
4. Are the users happy with the system, and committed to keep on using it?
5. Have arrangements been made for the equipment to be properly protected and serviced?
6. Are staff aware of precautions necessary for dealing with delicate electronic media, such as floppy disks?
7. Is the system secure?
8. Is your data secure? (Is there a chance of losing your sales debtor's list?)
9. Is there proper safeguard against disaster? (Would the loss of your sales debtor's list put you in danger of bankruptcy?)
10. How, and when, do you decide that the time has come to upgrade your system?

The items on the list fall into three main categories, system performance (items 1 - 4), system security (items 5 - 9), and future planning (item 10). Let's look at each of these areas separately.

System Performance

The customary way to assess whether a recently installed system is performing as expected is to carry out a **Post implementation review.** A review of this kind will highlight not only system performance matters, but also lessons to be learnt
for future system implementations, and may also throw up some system requirements that were missed out when the system was designed.

If you followed the advice in Chapter 6, and made a list of the objectives and benefits of implementing the system, you already have a yardstick to measure the effectiveness of the system. There are two main techniques for establishing whether the system has met expectations:

1. Interviewing staff using the system to establish attitudes and their subjective opinion on benefits of the system.
2. Performing quantitative analysis on system performance (such as time taken to process orders, size of backlog, no of staff required, etc.)

The results of a quantitative analysis are a solid indication to system performance. But don't allow successful results in this area to make you complacent about a negative staff attitude. Some resistance to change is natural, and will disappear when staff get used to the new system and see the benefits. The more that you have consulted with staff during the system development process, the quicker they will adapt to change and settle in to using the new system. If negative attitudes persist, you should deal with them quickly, as they can have a corrosive long term effect on motivation and productivity. To overcome a negative staff attitude, hold regular consultative meetings, find out where concern lies, and take whatever steps you can to meet these concerns. Where you are unable to meet their concerns, explain the reasons why.

If your quantitative analysis of the system shows discrepancies from the results that you expected, you will need to find out why. These might be a symptom of staff unwillingness to accept the system, an inadequate training programme, or a fault in your initial analysis. You should bear in mind that in the early stages of implementing a system, staff will be undergoing a **learning curve.** The speed at which people can operate a new procedure increases steadily with time, until it reaches a standard plateau (industrial engineers in manufacturing companies use a logarithmic formula to predict production targets for new products). If a failure to meet predicted performance targets is down to staff attitude, or poor training, it can be corrected (although you will have lost revenue in the meanwhile, and perhaps suffered a long term decline in credibility). If failure to perform is down to an incorrect analysis of the system, then you can only learn from your mistake, and try to think of fresh ways to achieve improvements.

In order to get the most out of the post implementation review, you should carry it out in four stages. The first stage will be almost immediately after implementation, and will concentrate on lessons to be learnt from the implementation itself. The second stage should be a few weeks after implementation, to ensure that staff are settling down into the new system, and to pick up any early lessons learnt. The third stage will be six months after implementation, when most of the benefits of the system should start to materialize. And the final stage of the review should take place a year or more after implementation, when the introduction of the system should be reviewed in the long term context of your business strategy. At each stage, you should compare the results of using the new system, against the objectives and benefits you initially predicted. The difference between the two is often surprising, and in many cases predicted benefits that did not materialize are often offset by unexpected benefits. For all the careful planning and flowcharting, systems implementation is not an exact science!

As a result of your post implementation review, you may come up with improvements to the system that can be implemented quite readily. In an environment where you are using mostly packaged software, making improvements of this sort will not generally lead to significant problems. If, however, part of your system has been developed using a 4GL (or similar package), don't rush into changes in an uncontrolled way. Many systems that are adapted and changed on a reactive basis end up being so butchered that they become bug-ridden and impossible to maintain.

System security

The most obvious security threat is the risk of losing your hardware. Computers, printers and other peripherals are expensive to replace. They should be physically secure, and well insured. And your loss does not stop at the cost of equipment. If a business is dependent upon a computer system, removal of facilities can have a devastating effect, both in terms of disruption, and in the ability to collect debts. It is not just the machinery that is important, it is the information held in it.

Many people who are fastidious in enforcing security for important ledgers or documents, seem blind to the need to protect information held in computer systems; even though a computer disk is nowhere near as robust as a ledger, and far more susceptible to damage. A missing page from a ledger is a problem, but a chink in a disk may result in the loss of all the information in several important ledgers.

Security considerations fall into three main areas:

1. Could third parties access confidential information on your system?
2. Could our storage media become lost or damaged?
3. If information is lost, are there adequate recovery procedures in place?

Many large companies have 'dial-up' lines to their mainframe computers. These present an opportunity for cunning enthusiasts (hackers) to break into systems and access highly confidential information. A small system with no connection to the telephone network, may not be under threat from hackers, but that doesn't mean it is secure.

Your PC does not have the benefit of the sophisticated, multi-layered security systems on corporate mainframes. The information held on your PC is an open book to anyone with a rudimentary knowledge of computers. If they can gain access to the PC, they will be able to gain access to the information held on it. So make sure that your systems are secure (most PCs have a keyboard lock key - this provides a simple and effective way of temporarily disabling your PC). And remember, valuable information is also held on floppy disks, which can easily be slipped into the pocket of a passing stranger. It is a good idea to use lockable cases for storing floppies, and to keep them out of sight. (Most of your information will be held permanently on hard disk, so you should not need to use floppies that often.)

Some applications require you to enter a password before gaining access. It is also possible to set up a simple 'front end' program that asks for a password when the PC is first switched on. These sort of systems do not present much of an obstacle to the experienced hacker, but can be useful for protecting sensitive information (such as salary details) from prying eyes in the office.

Theft is not the only way to lose information. Disks, especially floppy disks, are fragile, sensitive pieces of equipment that can easily be damaged. Information held on disks is encoded magnetically, and can be destroyed by strong electric or magnetic fields. So do not store disks near to electrical equipment. (There have been cases of disks becoming corrupted from electrical fields caused by disk drives! But it is doubtful whether this particular risk can be avoided!). Disks have been found to be corrupted following journeys on the underground. If you are transporting disks with valuable information, they can be shielded from electrical fields by wrapping in metal foil. Dust and grime presents a danger not only to the disk, but may cause expensive damage to your disk drives - so keep disks clean and physically protected at all times. Cleaning should also extend to the rest of your equipment. Special materials are available for cleaning keyboards and terminals: use the correct materials, and follow the instructions. If you have a significant amount of computer equipment, it may be worth asking for a quote from one of the specialized cleaning services that deal in computer cleaning. One of the biggest threats to hardware is the accidental spillage of a drink. Make it a firm rule that no drink or food is to be allowed near computers.

The greatest danger to a hard disk arises from movement of a PC. Make sure that desks or tables holding computers are solid, and will not shake when knocked. If you need to move a PC, find out if the hard disk must be **parked** first. Parking adjusts the disks so that the disk heads are positioned over a part of the disk which doesn't contain data. Some modern PCs (such as the 40Mbyte HP Vectra) park disks automatically, but many others do not.

Perhaps the most common cause of data loss is the one that shouldn't happen at all: accidental erasure. Commands such as **Erase *.***. or **Format c:**, have the effect of deleting all the files on your disk. Earlier versions of DOS would proceed with these commands without a moment's hesitation. But later versions use 'last chance' prompts, such as 'Are you sure?'. But this still isn't enough to prevent the determined kamikaze operator. Make sure that staff are fully aware of the implications of using these commands.

If the worse comes to the worse, there are methods for retrieving lost information. Because of the way DOS works, when a file is deleted, it is only part of the information pointing to where the file is stored that is removed, the information itself will not be written over until that part of the disk is needed. Several utilities make use of this, and allow the user to restore deleted files. Some packages are more sophisticated than others, in that they can even retrieve the remaining fragments of a file that has been written over. And some workshops have had success in retrieving information from physically damaged disks. If you need to resurrect information, the **Norton utilities** package provides a toolkit for the budding disk doctor. If you do 'lose' an important file on a disk, do not use that disk for anything else until you have tried to recover the lost file.

In a perfect world you should never need to resort to lazarean methods. All of your data should be methodically backed up on a daily basis. There are several methods of backing up data. The easiest way to make a backup copy of a file on your hard disk, is to copy it onto a floppy disk, and lock the floppy away. This system works fine for a single user who accesses relatively few files in a day. However, if you are running a busy office, it isn't feasible for each user to try and remember what they worked on and back it up to floppy. Even if they did, you would then have the problem of storing and filing the data. A solution to this is to backup the whole hard disk every day. Backing up a hard disk onto floppies takes a considerable amount of time; a better way is to use a **tape streamer**. A tape streamer backs up all the information on the hard disk onto a cassette tape. This tape can then be read back to reconstruct the hard disk if a fault occurs.

But backing up the whole disk can seem inefficient if you have altered only some files. And if your latest version contains an error, you could be backing up bad data by writing it over good. One way around these problems is to use an incremental backup facility. You can buy software that monitors what files have changed since the last backup, and only copies those. Incremental backup systems can work with floppy disks or tape streamers. Because your backups are limited to those files which have changes, you have the scope to maintain a longer historic record of your data.

Another factor to bear in mind is site loss, due to fire or other damage. A complete set of backups kept in the cupboard next to the computer is of little use if the office is destroyed. Backup copies should be taken off site at the very least weekly, and preferably daily. All backup copies of your programs should be kept off site.

If you do suffer extensive damage to your site, you will also be likely to suffer equipment loss. You need a plan to get your systems up and running as quickly as possible. You may need a replacement site. You should have contingency plans for acquiring replacement hardware, installing software, and reconstructing your data. Obviously, the items which take priority are those enabling staff to keep working productively, and your accounting system to bill customers. Hiring equipment may be a short term solution, but if this is part of your plans, you should try to obtain insurance cover for hire costs. Many companies insure the equipment value and forget about consequential loss and loss of profits insurance. Discuss these with your broker, to achieve the maximum possible protection.

Looking to the future

Once your system is installed and running successfully, the next upgrade to your system is probably the last thing you want to think about. But it is a problem you will need to address someday. And if you have followed the advice given in this book, hopefully, that day will be later rather than sooner.

When you listen to computer salesmen, you will hear much talk about the benefits of an **upgrade path**. A upgrade path is a way for your system to expand and grow, without the need for large amounts of your software to be abandoned and replaced.

One of the problems that IBM faced during the 1980s is that there was no natural upgrade between the various levels of hardware. At the bottom end of their product line was the PC XT/AT range running on DOS, and later OS/2. In the mid range were the System 36, System 38 machines, later replaced by the AS400, running another operating system. And at the top of the product range there were mainframes running under VM and MVS. This meant that software running on PCs could not be transferred (**ported**) to mini computers, and software running on mini computers could not be ported to mainframes. For large companies, which spend considerable time and effort developing and writing software this lack of compatibility was a major obstacle. One of the reasons for the increasing popularity of the C programming language over this period was the ease with which C programs could be converted to run under different operating systems on different machines. IBM has attacked the problem by developing standards for connecting systems. Several bodies embracing a wide range of manufacturers have attempted to define communication standards.

The most significant result of the drive to standardization has been the rise of the **Unix** operating system. Unix has always been closely associated with C, with most versions of Unix being written largely in C. Unix has the advantage of presenting a common interface across machines of various sizes, ranging from workstations to mainframes. Its success can be measured from the interest that IBM has shown in developing Unix - a sure sign that IBM regards it as a bandwagon they must keep up with.

Despite IBM's determination to push the OS/2 operating system, it is a fair bet that OS/2 will fail, and in a few years time the equivalent of today's PC will be a Unix workstation based on the Intel 80486 processor (or 80585, or 80686 or...).

But where does that leave you? Will DOS based systems be consigned to the scrap heap? For an answer look at the popularity of Amstrad's PCW range. They are based on the ancient CP/M operating system. But the widespread availability of software, and the low price of established technology have enabled the machines to cause a resurgence of interest in CP/M. People have started to write CP/M software again. The same will hold true for DOS five years from now, only more so. CP/M machines are chronically slow in comparison with today's AT compatibles. Not only do DOS based machines have the wide established base, they also have the power to meet the majority of user's needs.

There are two reasons why a company considers upgrading a system:

1. To increase the range of tasks which the system can carry out.
2. To increase the capacity of the system.

When we looked at assessing your needs in Chapter 3, we took the current volumes of information being processed, and multiplied by a factor of at least ten to get the capacity required for your system. This may have seemed excessive at the time, but experience shows that most companies outgrow their current requirements at a much quicker rate than expected. However, using a factor of ten should give you some confidence in meeting capacity requirements in the medium term When you do need extra capacity, it could mean that you need an upgrade in hardware. This can be an expensive option, as it may also require a change in operating system, and a change in software (another reason why our capacity estimates were taken on the safe side). Sometimes you will be lucky, and be able to meet the problem by investing in an extra disk drive. When you get to the stage where a hardware upgrade is required, you may be looking at a Unix solution, which will provide a more reliable long term upgrade path.

To increase the range of tasks handled by your system, you may be looking at buying an extra software package, or replacing a package that forms a module in your current system. Beware of an attack of 'featuritis'. Don't wait slavishly for every new release of your favourite software package, and buy it just to have the 'latest' version. If you have identified a need, look for a product that meets it. Don't go looking for new features, and then trying to find a need for them.

If you have followed the steps outlined in this book (identify needs → evaluate software → implement system) you should not be in a position where you 'need' new features for some time. However, you may have identified a potential direction for development; in the case of our example interior design company the LAN may be expanded considerably within a few years. But, as we have emphasized from time to time, systems development is an iterative process, and it is only when you start using the features of a product that you see the need for further features, which perhaps some other product has, but yours doesn't. *Don't swap packages in a hurry.* Often you will find that the other package doesn't have features that you find indispensable in your current system. Any change of package should be preceded with careful evaluation, and perhaps a trial for a few months. If you are considering a major upgrade, treat the whole process in the same way as you treated your initial implementation. Each step in the process is just as valid for an upgrade as it is for an initial implementation.

Summary of Chapter Eight - Maintaining and Upgrading Your System

System performance:

> Perform a post implementation review to assess whether your system is performing as expected
> Carry out quantitative analysis to ascertain whether your performance targets are being achieved.
> Interview staff to assess whether attitudes to and opinions of the new system are favourable.
> Take into account the learning curve necessary before staff become fully proficient with the new system.
> Don't rush to implement improvement requests as a result of your review. Plan carefully and consider the consequences first.

System security:

> A loss of equipment will cost you more than the replacement value. Disruption costs, and the inability to invoice customers will add greatly to your costs.
> Keep computers secure, and control third party access. Use the keyboard lock to disable unattended machines.
> Floppy disks must be kept away from electric and magnetic fields, and kept free of dust or grime. A foil shield can protect disks in transit.
> Computer equipment should be cleaned regularly, using the correct special materials.
> No food or drink should be allowed near computers.
> Passwords can be used to protect sensitive applications, general access to machines (unlikely to be effective against a serious hacker).
> Keep PCs on solid desks. Park hard disks before moving.
> Be careful with **Erase *.***, and **Format c:**.
> Use norton utilities, or a similar package to restore lost data.
> Always back up your data.
> Backup by copying onto floppy, using a tape streamer to back up the whole disk, or using an incremental backup program.
> Keep backups off-site (especially programs) to safeguard against fire, or other site loss.
> Have contingency plans for reconstructing your system in the event of site loss.
> Insure for consequential loss and loss of profits to cover equipment hire charges and disruption costs.

Looking to the future:

Reasons for upgrading are to add new features or increase capacity.
Don't rush into changing a package without extensive evaluation and
trial.
Treat a major system upgrade as a system implementation - the
steps are the same.

CHAPTER 9

Conclusion

We have covered a lot of ground in this book. Let's review the major stages, before we finish with a few key principles.

Assess your needs first. Think of your real underlying needs, not of procedures that you have always followed. Start from first principles. What are your goals for the company? What is your strategy at the highest level? Forget your current system. Break down your strategic objectives into a list of business needs. Use these as your starting point.

Form a 'pyramid of objectives' that build up into your strategic aims. This is your check list for what the system must do.

When you have your objectives, decide what inputs and outputs the system must have, and sketch out the desired information flow. Your system must be consistent with your needs. It is designed to support those needs. Be creative! Don't be constrained by what you think is possible. Go for what you ideally want.

For each category of information, estimate the current volume of data processed by your company. Separate data into standing data and transaction data.

At this stage you have a logical model for the business system. From this you should be able to tell what sort of hardware will support your system.

Mentally break up your logical model into separate modules. Try and find a mix of software packages that corresponds with these modules. The fewer modules the better. The strain on the system comes from the interfaces. The fewer the interfaces, the more efficient the system. If you cannot find the right packages, consider developing some of the system yourself using a 4GL.

Avoid relying on utility packages. Your interfaces will proliferate! Always go for the integrated solution.

When you have a proposed physical system, sketch it out and go through each interface in your head. Look for difficulties. Your physical system should be a reflection of your logical model. Write out a system specification. List objectives and benefits.

What if one PC isn't enough? The efficiency of a hardware configuration depends on how users want to share data. If many users want to access the same database, consider a multi-user, single-processor system. If most users have their own data, consider a LAN.

Plan the implementation meticulously. Never go ahead with a live system until you have thoroughly tested the new system, preferably using a parallel run. Do not skimp on training.

When the system is installed, carry out a post implementation review. Compare your findings with the objectives and benefits anticipated in the system specification.

Two principles that you should always follow:

1. Consult with your staff at all stages, and respond to their need where you can. Their commitment is vital to a successful system.
2. The driving sequence is Needs-Software-Hardware. Whenever you are in doubt, go back to first principles and ask: What am I really trying to achieve?

System development is an iterative process. On paper it looks like a science, but in practice it is an art. Black and white smudges into grey, and subjective judgements replace clinical evaluation. Going round in circles is inevitable. But when the time is right, you must break out and take a decision. If one of your major objectives is threatened, then you *must* delay and solve the problem. Otherwise, once your system is substantially in line with your initial list of needs, then you must press ahead.

The most indispensable requirement, which is often sadly lacking, is common sense, Or, to put it another way, a sense of perspective. Computer systems are such technically intricate things that it is easy to get bogged down in detail. Always stand back and ask the basic questions. And keep standing back at regular intervals. In short, think like a businessman, and not like a programmer. Now that shouldn't be too difficult. Should it?

Appendix A - Binary and Hexadecimal Numbers

In all conventional counting systems, when we run out of numbers, we move one space to the left to generate higher numbers. For example, in the decimal system, when we reach nine, we need to start to start a new column to the left to make ten. Then when we reach ninety nine, we need to move to the left again to make one hundred. The way this system works leads to an interesting fact. Each column to the left represents a power of ten.

$$10 \qquad = 10^1$$
$$100 \qquad = 10 \times 10 = 10^2$$
$$1000 \qquad = 10 \times 10 \times 10 = 10^3$$

Similarly, in a binary number each space to the left represents a power of two. You can convince yourself of this by comparing the workings below with the numbers in Table A1.

$$0010 \qquad = 2^1 = 2$$
$$0100 \qquad = 2^2 = 4$$
$$1000 \qquad = 2^3 = 8$$
$$1011 \qquad = 2^3 + 2^1 + 2^0$$
$$\qquad \qquad = 8 + 2 + 1$$
$$\qquad \qquad = 11$$

For people working with computers, it is advantageous to have a more compact way of representing binary numbers. Unfortunately, simply translating binary numbers into decimal is not a convenient option. To see why this is, consider the binary number 1001 1010. The second part of the number, 1010 is equivalent to the number 10 in decimal. The first part of the number (taken in isolation) is equivalent to the number 9 in decimal. But to get the decimal equivalent of the complete binary number, we cannot simply take 9 and 10 and put them together to get 910. Instead, we have to work out the decimal equivalent of the whole number:

Table A1. - Different counting systems.

Decimal	Binary	Hexadecimal
1	0001	1
2	0010	2
3	0011	3
4	0100	4
5	0101	5
6	0110	6
7	0111	7
8	1000	8
9	1001	9
10	1010	A
11	1011	B
12	1100	C
13	1101	D
14	1110	E
15	1111	F
16	10000	10

$$1001\ 1010 = 2^7 + 2^4 + 2^3 + 2^1 = 128 + 16 + 8 + 2 = 154$$

In order to avoid this messy conversion process, people working with computers have come up with a different way of representing binary bumbers. Consider the third column in Table A1. Instead of counting in groups of ten or groups of two, this system counts in groups of sixteen. Because there are only ten digits available in our conventional system (0 to 9), the letters A to F have been used to represent the extra six digits. This system is called the Hexadecimal system.

Why is it an advantage to count in groups of sixteen? From Table A1, you can see that the hexadecimal number 10 is equivalent to the binary number 10000 (both of which are equivalent to 16 in decimal). The 'carry over' column (when you have to start using an extra column to the left, i.e. at the number 10) in hexadecimal coincides with the fourth 'carry over' column in binary. Because of this, a binary number can be converted to hexadecimal by taking each group of four binary digits in turn and converting them separately.

Let's take our example binary number, 1001 1010. From Figure 2.5, you can see that the hexadecimal for 1001 is 9, and the hexadecimal for 1010 is A; therefore, the hexadecimal for 1001 1010 is 9A. (You can prove this by converting 9A to decimal, (9X16) + 10 = 144 + 10 = 154, the same answer as when we converted 1001 1010 to decimal.) Using this system, even very long binary numbers can be converted quickly to hexadecimal by breaking down the binary number into groups of four and converting them separately.

People working with computers rarely use binary numbers, even though computers can work with nothing else. It is far more convenient to use hexadecimal, referred to by those in the know as simply 'hex'. Hexadecimal numbers are usually denoted by a trailing h, so a number written as 9Ah is 9A in hexadecimal, equivalent to 1001 1010 in binary or 154 in decimal.

Appendix B - Step by step execution of a program

When the computer is instructed to run a program, the program is copied from the Disk where it is stored into memory. In Figure B1, a program has been copied into memory, and occupies space starting at memory address 0100h. Each memory address has a length of eight bits, which we know is one byte.

Once the program has been copied into memory, the CPU will start to execute the program. The first byte of the program is copied from memory and transferred to the CPU. Because there are eight bits in a byte, eight wires are needed to transfer one byte of information simultaneously. This pathway of parallel wires is called a Bus. The first byte of memory is passed down the Data Bus to the CPU. The CPU interprets the first byte of the program as an instruction code.

In the case of our example (the Z80 chip), the binary code 0011 1010 is an instruction that tells the chip to load the A register with the contents of the memory address specified by the two bytes following. So, the CPU will look at the following two bytes; 0000 0001 and 0001 0000. Together these give the required memory address. We can translate this to hex (taking each group of four at a time), giving us the hex address 0110. So, the first three bytes of the program tell the CPU to load the A register with the contents of memory address 0110h. From Figure B1, you can see that address 0110h holds the number 0000 0001. This number will be loaded into the A register.

The first instruction is now complete. Because the first instruction has used up three bytes of memory (one for the instruction itself, and two to specify the required address), the CPU knows that it has to look at memory location 103h for its next instruction. The binary code 0010 0001 is an instruction to the CPU to load the HL pair of registers with the two binary numbers following. So, the HL registers are loaded with the numbers 0000 0001 and 0001 0001.

That instruction has used up three bytes, so the CPU moves on to memory location 106h for its next instruction. The code at location

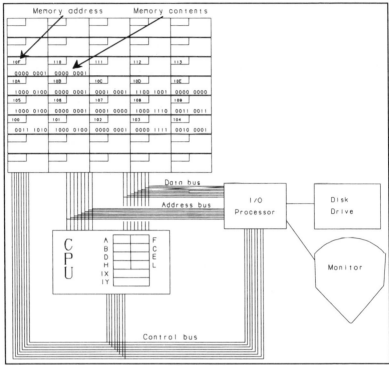

Figure B1

106h; 1000 1110, is an instruction to the CPU to add the contents of the memory address specified by the HL registers to the contents of the A register. The memory location specified by the HL registers is 0000 0001 0001 0001, which is 0111h in hex. Looking at Figure B1, you can see that the number held at memory address 0111h is 0000 0001. So the CPU adds this number to the number already held in the A register (if you look back, you can see that the previous number in the A register was also 0000 0001).

This instruction has only used up one byte of memory, so the CPU looks at memory location 107h for its next instruction. The binary code 0011 0010 is an instruction to the CPU to place the contents of the A register at the memory address specified by the two bytes following: 0000 0001 0001 0010, or, translating to hex, 0112h.

On completing this instruction, the CPU moves on to the next instruction at address 10Ah. This instruction, 1100 1001, tells the CPU to finish executing the program.

So after all that, what have we achieved? If you have followed carefully you should have noticed that we have taken the number 1 from memory location 110h, and placed it in the A register. Then we have added the number 1, from memory location 111h to the A register. We have then taken the result and placed it at memory location 112h.

The upshot of our program is that it adds together the numbers 1 and 1. Not a very useful program! And worse, it does not even display the result where we might see it!

But hopefully, going through the program in this way has given you some insight into the way the computer works.

Appendix C - Software Reviews

Word Processors

Wordperfect, by Sentinel software, has firmly established itself as the market leader. The product is rich in features, and later versions can handle graphics in a way that surpasses the capabilities of any other product in the market place.

The product has an extensive spelling checker, a well constructed (though relatively slim) thesaurus, facilities for sorting columns into alphabetic order, and for carrying out mathematical calculations imbedded in the text. Paragraph formatting (such as numbered paragraphs, hanging indents) comes easily, and commonly used features such as bold lettering and underlining are switched on and off using function keys.

Wordperfect shows the minimum of on-screen messages, just a single line at the bottom stating the name of the document, page number and cursor position. But no benefit is lost, the clean screen makes using the product feel like typing on an ordinary sheet of paper: a much more comfortable feeling than being presented with complicated ruler lines and a long list of obscure options. Help is always at hand: the product is supplied with a sturdy, plastic, keyboard, help template, and a function key allows instant access to help screens. The help screens are concise, but this is not necessarily a disadvantage, the pressed user becomes annoyed when wading through screens of verbiage to locate the answer to a simple question. One area where the help facility does fall down, is in the absence of tracking help, a loss that will particularly affect the new user. But there are other features which compensate, notably the provision of an on-line tutorial and a work book.

The documentation is reasonable, but not impressive. It mainly consists of a dictionary of commands in alphabetic order, and could be improved if organized by function (some might regard this a debatable case). But, again the deficiency in the documentation is partly compensated by the provision of the workbook and on-line tutorial. (A proper user's guide would make a big difference.)

The outline facility provided is hardly worthy of the name, being little more than a paragraph numbering device. Another gripe is in the handling of printers and character sets. Laser printers are well catered for, but setting up the software to correctly drive a daisywheel with a sheet feeder is difficult, to say the least. Wordperfect claim to have simplified handling of printers in recent versions, but it seems there is still room for improvement.

But the faults do little to dent the vast lead that Wordperfect has established over comparable products in the market place. In summary, despite a few irritating omissions, Wordperfect deserves its position as market leader. And, if you need a quality word processor, it is worth the price.

If Wordperfect is the new king of the roost, Micropro's **Wordstar** must rank as the deposed monarch. Unrivalled in its day, and still a force to be reckoned with, it has been dragged into the 1980s with the addition of all the fashionable features: graphics, thesaurus, proportional spacing. But Micropro market two versions of Wordstar: a graphics version (Wordstar 2000), and a version for heavy text processing (Wordstar professional). This isn't a great deal of use for people who want to combine the facilities of both. Many people born and bred on Wordstar will continue to support the product, but new users will find better value elsewhere.

Microsoft's **Word** is the other major contender in the heavyweight word processor stakes. Although it doesn't compete overall with Wordperfect, it scores important hits in some areas, and might suit some users better. The outliner is good and works with word's style sheets option to automatically select different styles for headings at corresponding levels. It does not, however, have anything like the graphics capabilities of Wordperfect, and paragraph formatting, although flexible, is clumsy to operate.

There are a number of other word processors in the same price range as these three, but many of them represent poor value for money. At the lower end of the market, Arnor's **Protext** is a fast word processor with many advanced features. Innova software's **Topcopy plus** has attracted much favourable comment. Both of these are worth considering. One word of caution, if you are considering a budget word processor, don't rely on the word of a salesman. Make sure that the product has had at least two good reviews, and insist on seeing it work using the same computer-printer configuration that you will be using before you buy.

Spreadsheets

The three major contenders in the spreadsheet market are **Lotus 123, Supercalc,** and **Quattro.**

Lotus 123 is firmly established as the market leader. As you would expect, it is a competent product, with a full range of features. The product claims to be a combined spreadsheet/database/graphics package. But this should be taken with a pinch of salt; 123's graphics and database capabilities are no better than are available on rival spreadsheets. Until recent versions, the graphics were frankly appalling, but this has now been addressed. The product comes in a solid package, with full documentation: a getting started book, a tutorial, and a reference manual. The biggest single fault with the product is that it is copy protected (i.e. a special coding system ensures that you cannot make more than one working copy of the program at any one time). Copy protected programs are bad news: if you have a disk problem you may not be able to get the program up and running again. If you are thinking of getting a spreadsheet, Lotus 123 has all the facilities that you would ever need. But so do other, less expensive, programs with no copy protection.

Supercalc, by Computer Associates, is a long standing rival to 123, with a similar array of features. Later versions boast the availability of add-in software, thus enabling other packages to work in close harmony with Supercalc. But in practice this chiefly refers to CA's own database package, Silverado, thus confirming the current trend for spreadsheet packages to become more database like.

Borland's Quattro is much cheaper than 123 or Supercalc, but it is by no means a watered down package. Quattro has all the features of its elder brothers, and in many areas outperforms them. It has just about every function you could think of, including matrix multiplication and operations on selected groups. The graphics facility produces superb output on a VGA (i.e. high resolution colour) screen, and facilities are included for exporting graphs to a word processor (the example pie chart and histogram used in Chapter 4 were produced by Quattro). The manuals are particularly helpful, including a 'getting started' book, a user guide, and a reference manual. If you decide that you need a spreadsheet package, it would be difficult to find a reason *not* to pick this one.

Databases

First we'll look at language based systems.

We have already used Ashton Tate's **dBase** in several examples in Chapter 4 With the advent of relational language standards, dBase is showing its age. It is fighting back with the inclusion of an SQL option, but the implementation is untidy. You have the choice to use one language standard or the other, but cannot easily combine the two. Recent versions also include special facilities to speed up the development of applications and reports (a menu based 'application generator'), and these are obviously a response to new products becoming available in the PC market (see Oracle below). The recently introduced 'control centre' as a front end to the product is an effort to compete with the menu based products, but the menus are by no means intuitive for the new user. Ashton Tate may be fighting on too many fronts at once, but faced with the prospect of a declining market share they have to do something. Still, anyone who wants a serious database system, whether for building applications, or purely to have quick, flexible power over information, cannot go too far wrong with dBase. But don't place your order too quickly...

A product in the same category as dBase, better known in the USA than in the UK, is **Rbase**. Rbase has a much better designed SQL interface than dBase, and generally provides relational facilities which are easier to access.

If you are committed to the dBase language standard, the dBase clones **Clipper**, and **Foxbase**, offer similar functionality to dBase (sometimes better) at a cheaper price.

Many market leaders are used to competition developing from new young companies, but Ashton Tate has a more frightening spectre looking over its shoulder. Oracle corporation, which boasts itself as the largest database software company in the world, originally sold its **Oracle** database product in the mainframe/mini market, but is now pushing hard at the PC market. The product has always been SQL based, and it is fair to say that SQL has achieved much of its prominence through Oracle rather than the other way round. When Oracle first entered the PC market, the product was priced beyond what most small businesses would call a sensible level (it was targeted at the corporate PC user who wanted to link to mainframe database systems).

But Oracle has started to offer price sweeteners which bring it into the small businessman's range. However it is a hungry product, requiring over 2 megabytes of memory, and many small businesses would need to upgrade their machines to be able to run the system. Nevertheless, it offers all the facilities that any serious database user could want, and it looks to be the product of the future.

At the low-price end of the market is Megatech's **Tas+**. Billed as a relational database system (it isn't in the strict sense of the word), Tas+ is a language based system controlled by menus! Despite these apparent contradictions, Tas+ is powerful enough to develop sophisticated applications. It includes application development tools similar to (if not as powerful as) those found in dBase and Oracle. The documentation is not well designed, but looking at the price, it seems churlish to get too picky. If you feel you need the flexibility of a language based system, without the pain of a dBase sized bill Tas+ is worth looking at.

Of the menu based systems, Sapphire software's **Dataease** heads the market, coming second after dBase in the overall ratings. Although it can be maddeningly frustrating to go through many steps to answer a simple query (c.f. the comparison in Table 4.1), menu based systems do have their uses, and Dataease is a well thought out product that is not only easy to use, but also hides powerful language capabilities (accessed through the advanced report builder). The product allows you to design new menus, and customize the standard menus. It would be a good choice if you wanted to implement, for example, a query system that would be accessed occasionally by several people. A feature that might appeal to the security conscious is the requirement to enter a name and password before you can use the product. If you feel that you need a menu based system, Dataease is a good, if expensive choice.

There are other packages on the market, some at significantly lower costs than the packages mentioned here. But few cheap packages are rich in features (one exception being Tas+). However, it is a changing market, and if you wish to buy a database package on a budget, keep a close eye on the magazine reviews.

Paint and Draw Packages

As regards products in the market place, Microsoft's **Paintbrush** is a well established paint type of program, Digital Research's **Gem Draw**

Plus is a reasonable drawing package, if limited. However, those involved in design might take a look at Digital Research's latest offering, **Gem Artline**; it has the flexibility of a paint package, but is in fact object based. Objects can be manipulated easily, and it can produce high quality text in various styles and sizes. There is no doubt that it is an excellent program, which probably explains the high price. Another package in the Artline mould is **Correl Draw**, this has attracted some very favourable reviews, and can't be ignored if you need software in this class.

There are many CADD packages on the market, **Autocadd**, is at the top end, with a price to match; **Fastcadd**, is a strong challenger, at a cheaper price. Generic Software's **Cadd** claims to be the biggest selling package. Sensibly, Generic offers the software at different levels, so that light users do not have to pay for features they don't need. (Many of the diagrams in this book were produced using Generic Cadd.)

Several products on the market combine the features of both 'presentation graphics' and 'management graphics' packages, notably **Draw Applause** from Ashton Tate, and **Harvard Graphics** from Software Publishing. Both are worth looking at if you need this type of product.

Integrated Packages

In the market place there are some surprisingly cheap packages available, for example, **ABLE-1** from Able International. But, apart from a few gimmicks, the product has sparse facilities, is poorly implemented, and the word processor is horrid. On the other hand, Logotron's **Eight-in-one**, though hardly rich in features, at least has a usable word processor, and the features that it has are useful and easy to use. And Eight-in-one is cheaper than Able. But neither of these packages will stand up well to demanding business use.

In the mid-range of the market, Migent's **Ability Plus** has all the specifications on paper to make it look great value for money. And indeed, in many areas it has powerful well integrated features. But the word processor lets it down badly.

At the top end of the market, the products in contention are: **Smart** from Informix, Lotus's **Symphony**, and Ashton Tate's **Framework**.

Smart is a solid, traditional style package. Although you don't get the equivalent of say, Wordperfect, Lotus 123, and dBase, you do get reliable packages, which meet the majority of an office's needs. You also get the smart programming language, which the adventurous user could use to produce mini-applications. Smart is not strong on integration ,and doesn't communicate easily with other software. But on the plus side, it doesn't place great requirements on your hardware. Smart is offered at a wide range of prices, so if you are considering buying it, it is worth shopping around.

Symphony comes from a stable renowned for a spreadsheet package, and it shows. When you first use the package you might think you've started the wrong program, up comes the spreadsheet grid just like 123. A curious place to start for an 'integrated package'. Like many packages (123 and Framework included), Symphony requires any working document to be held entirely in memory; this is an unwelcome restriction on a package where the spelling checker and outline facilities must also be run as memory resident 'add-in's. The word processor has all the standard features, with no obvious bugs or omissions (but nothing to inspire you). The spreadsheet, as you would expect, is full featured. The database system is pretty limited, offering basically what you would expect to get from one of the cheaper 'card index' style packages. Symphony includes a 'programming' capability, enabling you to build mini-applications. But the absence of any relational features in the database must place a strain on what can be achieved comfortably. All in all a fairly ordinary package. But not, unfortunately, an ordinary price.

Ashton Tate's Framework is as much a concept as it is a software package. When you use the product, you work in 'frames' (windows displayed on the screen). You can have many frames open at once, and can move between them. This means that you can run concurrent sessions on the database, spreadsheet and word processor at the same time. A frame can contain other frames, and links can be established between frames. In practice, this means that you can build up a powerful and flexible system. Framework also includes communications facilities and a built-in language, FRED (FRamework EDiting language). The language is sufficiently powerful to build applications, but they do not execute at lightning speed. The biggest drawback is Framework's requirement that all working files have to be held in memory, making a machine with extended memory highly recommended if you deal with any volume of data (the alternative is to configure a section of the hard disk as 'virtual' memory, which slows the system down). In summary, Framework is a competent and intriguing product, and if your requirements boil down to a standard word processing, spreadsheet, and database package, it probably provides a novel, satisfactory solution.

Appendix D - IBM compatible PCs

This section gives a brief review of machines likely to be of use to a businessman considering buying a computer for the first time.

All the machines in this section are essentially copies of IBM machines, so we should at least give IBM a mention. However, buying IBM is unlikely to be a good strategy for the small businessman. Large corporate buyers have their reasons for paying IBM prices (there is a famous quote, 'Nobody got fired for buying IBM'), but the small businessman would be well advised to look at the clone market.

You may have reservations about buying a 'copy', but be assured many of the copies available today are far superior to the original products that they emulate. Yes, you do have to be careful at the 'bargain basement' end of the market. But there are a select group of manufacturers that produce highly respected products at reasonable prices.

The biggest, and best known clone manufacturer is **Compaq**. The deskpro range is a fine example of good design and engineering. But Compaq have started to cash in on their market position in recent years, and their prices do not look so competitive now that the market has widened. In addition, they sell through dealers, which means that a generous margin for the dealer has to be found.

One company has avoided the problem of finding a dealer commission by dealing direct with the customer. **Dell**, the Texas based company founded by young whizz kid Michael Dell in 1984, has grown to become America's seventh largest PC manufacturer in four years. How have Dell done it? By producing a high quality machine, and selling it by mail order! Sounds like a funny way to sell a high-tec product, but Dell offer a no-quibble guarantee and a superb support package to compensate for the lack of face to face contact. And there is one other thing, because they don't pay dealers, they are able to undercut IBM and Compaq by up to 40%.

Another company with a reputation for producing well designed machines at a reasonable price is **Apricot**. They were the first to produce a 386 based clone, based on IBM's new MCA design standard, and recently, have launched a 486 machine intended as a file server. Apricot also include some interesting innovations in their machines, built-in security features and support for running PCs on a network (see LANs above).

For the businessman on the move, a portable computer may solve the paperwork problem. Excellent machines are produced by **Compaq, Zenith,** and **Toshiba**. Compaq produce the 'quality' machine, although Zenith probably represent better value for money. Toshiba were the early leaders in the portable market, their gas plasma screens have excellent resolution but are not very bright, and sometimes can be difficult to see. For true portability Toshiba produce the smallest IBM compatible, but this machine has only one floppy disk drive, which most serious users are likely to find too limiting.

On a tight budget? **Amstrad**'s machines are difficult to beat on price. And Amstrad don't achieve their competitive prices by skimping on design. Their machines pack more power into a smaller space than IBM's original machines. But it is fair to see that Amstrad's machines do rely heavily on plastic, and don't have the robust construction of a Dell or a Compaq. But if you are keeping a close watch on costs, and you don't intend to throw your computer around the office, Amstrad provides the machine for you. For the wary shopper, Opus provide comparative machines in the same price range.

The machine you buy, will depend on your requirements. We take a detailed look at how you arrive determine the minimum specifications for your requirements in Chapter 6. Here are some suggestions for the leading contenders in each class.

For a fast, reliable all-round performer, with excellent back-up and guaranteed 24 hour on-site maintenance, the Dell 220 is a machine to suit most needs (this book was produced using a Dell 220).

The power hungry user, with more interest in performance than cost will look to the Compaq Desqpro 386/33. The machine combines several advanced features to produce unrivalled performance in the PC compatible class. A machine that might catch your interest is the Mac II, and you should at least see a demonstration of the Mac, before making a decision.

The man on the move might consider the Zenith Supersport range. These machines have proved very popular, and are available over a wide price/performance range.

Appendix E - Recommended Printers

If you are looking for a daisywheel printer, **Juki**, **Brother**, and **Qume**, all make reasonable machines, covering a variety of prices. The price is usually determined by the print speed. Around 20 characters per second (cps) is slow, but acceptable; 50 cps is reasonable for a daisywheel. If you wish to use an automatic sheet feeder, make sure that you see it working without trouble for at least 30 sheets, using your stationery before you buy. (Sheet feeders are notorious for not working.)

If you are going for a dot matrix printer, a 24 pin model is preferable to a 9 pin. A very good range is offered by **NEC**. Other manufacturers worth considering are **Epson** (who initially set the standards in the dot matrix market), or, if cost is important, **Amstrad**. Most software assumes that dot matrix printers are Epson-compatible, so whatever printer you choose, make this a requirement.

If you need laser printer speed and quality, the **Hewlett Packard**, have set the standards in this area, and many dealers offer competitive prices on the **Laserjet II** range. However, **Qume**'s **Crystalprint** range offers alternative technology which delivers the same performance at a lower price. For the space conscious, the Crystalprint is an ideal choice, it has a compact, square shape, with no overhanging paper trays.

Most software expects laser printers to be compatible with the Laserjet II or accept **Postscript** commands (Postscript is a widely accepted page description language). *Do not buy a laser printer if it does not support either of these standards.* Postscript provides greater flexibility, is device independent, and uses a system where images can be scaled without loss of quality. Postscript files can be transferred to professional typesetting equipment and produced to publication standard. However, postscript printers are generally a lot more expensive, and are probably not worth the extra expense, unless you have a need for high quality document production. Also, postscript printers can only be used with software that supports postscript output (most other types of printer can at least print out an ASCII file).

If you want to produce documents with colour, a reasonably priced option is the Hewlett Packard **Paintjet**, which produces coloured output at 180 dots per inch. The Paintjet also has the advantage that text and graphics can be mixed on the same page. The Paintjet can be very slow, when printing documents containing a high graphic content, but it still represents good value at the price.

For high quality graphics, the **Mitsubishi** thermal printer produces 300 dot per inch quality, but at a heavy cost in terms of price and speed. **Tektronix** specialize in high quality colour reproduction, and produce a range of printers of various types. High speed, high quality colour printers are available, but these are very expensive, and should not be considered without taking specialist advice. (The alternative way to produce high quality colour output, is to use a plotter.)

Appendix F - ASCII Codes

Code in Hex	Code in Decimal	Character	Code in Hex	Code in Decimal	Character
00	0		38	56	8
|	|		39	57	9
to	to	Special	3A	58	:
|	|	chars.	3B	59	;
|	|		3C	60	<
1F	31		3D	61	=
20	32	(space)	3E	62	>
21	33	!	3F	63	?
22	34	"	40	64	@
23	35	#	41	65	A
24	36	$	42	66	B
25	37	%	43	67	C
26	38	&	44	68	D
27	39	'	45	69	E
28	40	(	46	70	F
29	41	)	47	71	G
2A	42	*	48	72	H
2B	43	+	49	73	I
2C	44	,	4A	74	J
2D	45	-	4B	75	K
2E	46	.	4C	76	L
2F	47	/	4D	77	M
30	48	0	4E	78	N
31	49	1	4F	79	O
32	50	2	50	80	P
33	51	3	51	81	Q
34	52	4	52	82	R
35	53	5	53	83	S
36	54	6	54	84	T
37	55	7	55	85	U

Code in Hex	Code in Decimal	Character	Code in Hex	Code in Decimal	Character
56	86	V	7E	126	~
57	87	W	7F	127	DEL
58	88	X		(special character,	
59	89	Y		delete)	
5A	90	Z			
5B	91	[			
5C	92	\			
5D	93	]			
5E	94				
5F	95				
60	96	`			
61	97	a			
62	98	b			
63	99	c			
64	100	d			
65	101	e			
66	102	f			
67	103	g			
68	104	h			
69	105	i			
6A	106	j			
6B	107	k			
6C	108	l			
6D	109	m			
6E	110	n			
6F	111	o			
70	112	p			
71	113	q			
72	114	r			
73	115	s			
74	116	t			
75	117	u			
76	118	v			
77	119	w			
78	120	x			
79	121	y			
7A	122	z			
7B	123	{			
7C	124					
7D	125	}			

Index